THE SUPER BEINGS

by John Randolph Price

ARNAN PUBLISHING
INCORPORATED   Austin, Texas

The Superbeings, Copyright @ 1981 by John Randolph Price

Library of Congress Catalog Card Number 81-71026
International Standard Book Number 0-94-2082-00-1

Arnan Publishing
3601 Far West Blvd.
Austin, Texas 78731

Printed in the United States of America
Cover design by J. Don Evans

This book is dedicated to
YOU
and to all who are seeking
"the license of a higher order of beings."

Acknowledgment

The author wishes to express deepest gratitude and appreciation to the men and women of Superbeings Ltd. for their loving support and inspiration.

For you ". . . a lamp will not be wanting and a shepherd will not fail, and a fountain will not dry up."

CONTENTS

INTRODUCTION

It has been said that behind all fiction is a basis of fact. Does this mean that there is a grain of truth in the fictional **Superman**? What did the original creator of this comic strip and movie character have in mind when he first conceived the idea? Did he intuitively believe that man may someday evolve into a super-human creature with "out-of-this-world" powers?

If so, he was right.

There is documented evidence that man has the ability (the power), and has demonstrated it, to read minds, foretell the future, materialize form, transcend time and space, communicate with other forms of life, and control the elements. Newspapers have chronicled feats of incredible strength—far beyond the capacity of "humanhood"—and super-intelligence has been the fascinating study of scholars and researchers for centuries.

Of even greater importance, however, is the fact that certain men and women on earth have discovered the

secret of total harmonious living, where there is no ill-ness or aging, lack or limitation, failure or futility.

Would you not call these individuals **Superbeings**? And what is it that gives them these super-human characteristics?

Modern science reports that the entire universe is made up of energy. The illumined Ones tell us that this Energy is in reality the One Presence and Power of the universe—all-Knowing, all-Loving, everywhere-present —and that this pure Mind Energy is individualized in man, *as* man. This truth has been realized by men and women in all walks of life, and they are rapidly evolving toward undreamed of powers. A few have reached the point of mastery, and they are living on earth now, dem-onstrating what we all can and must become.

They say to all, "you live in this world, but you are not of it. You are from a higher realm, with only a spark of remembrance in your deeper mind of all that you once were, and can be again. You must fan that spark. You must awaken to the Power within you—not only for yourself, but for the good of all mankind."

The truth is, man by himself is simply a victim of cir-cumstances, but when linked with the Power, all things are possible. He enters a new realm of Energy that is so superior to his so-called human consciousness that his actions will stagger the imagination of the average per-son.

Volumes could be written about people on the Path and their demonstrations achieved in the various stages of consciousness development . . .

- Terminal cancer has "miraculously" disappeared with-out a trace.

- The blind have seen again.

- So-called permanently withered limbs have grown strong and normal.

- A business in a state of ruin suddenly attracts an avalanche of customers with mushrooming sales and profits.

- Capital required to start a new business is brought forth by a stranger when all the banks said no.

- The steering wheel of an automobile moving at high speed is "mysteriously" taken over by unseen hands, enabling the vehicle to avoid a serious accident.

- A lonely woman affirms the right mate and attracts the ideal man at a "chance" meeting.

- The word is spoken for gasoline when a car runs out of fuel in the middle of the desert and suddenly the tank is full.

- An orange grove in a severe freeze is visualized surrounded by a warm light and is totally protected from harm.

- A plane out of control is safely landed after the wife of a man on board sensed the perilous situation and affirmed his deliverance.

- A young woman confined to bed with multiple sclerosis is healed with the realization that "God is my health, I can't be sick."

- A criminal serving a life sentence is suddenly spiritually renewed through contemplation of his Inner Self, and within weeks is released to live a new life filled with service to others.

- A horribly burned hand is instantly healed.

- A school teacher daily affirms "true place" and finds a new career in sales with earnings in excess of $100,000 a year.

- A salesman struggles to make ends meet until he "discovers" through meditation a highly-developed creative consciousness for inventions. His machines now play a major role in the productivity of American industry.

- A retailer experiencing a declining business gives himself a "prosperity treatment" several times a day resulting in such an increase in business that he opens four additional stores.

- A writer whose articles were regularly rejected begins affirming that his Higher Self is writing through him—now *all* of his writings are being accepted.

- A businessman credits the building of a major multi-million dollar company within a short period of time to the daily practice of creative imagination, seeing in his mind's eye the giant corporate complex he desired.

- A real estate agent doubled, then tripled, her already substantial income by daily affirming prosperous conditions for all people, herself included.

A failure finds success, the poor become rich, the sick become well, the lonely find companionship, a family is united, a marriage is healed, a troublesome legal situation vanishes, the answer to a problem is given, the endangered are protected.

As Paracelsus said, ". . . could we rightly comprehend the mind of man, nothing would be impossible to us upon the earth."

That's what this book is all about.

AUTHOR'S PREFACE:

The Search Begins

On a Friday evening in January 1967, while looking through the bookshelves in our den for something to read, I was literally forced to pick up a book written by one of my clients. I had thumbed through the book months before with little interest, but when I picked it up again the book opened to a page where the author was discussing man's relationship to God. He said that God wants man to be happy—that it is God's will for man to be successful, prosperous and totally fulfilled—and that nothing will be impossible to man once he learns to co-operate with his inner Resources. This was a new realization for me and I thought about it all week-end.

There had been some discontent in my life during the previous year, but I couldn't put my finger on any particular cause for the dissatisfaction. My marriage and family life were very happy and fulfilling, we were active in our church, I was executive vice president of a Chicago advertising agency, and from all appearances I was considered highly successful. But I had that nagging feeling that there was more to life than I was experiencing— that there was a greater degree of livingness, a higher level of fulfillment "out there" somewhere. In fact, my prayers usually went something like—"God, there must be more . . . help me to find what I'm looking for, *whatever it may be.*"

I know that I was guided to pick up that book, and when I left for the office on Monday I asked my wife to go to the library and check out any books she could find that might give us more insight into this "new" idea of man's relationship to God. When I came home that night there was a stack of metaphysical books on the table.

My personal notes from that period of time reveal some of the thoughts that stimulated and inspired us:

God cannot withhold good. It is against His nature.

Whatever you affirm and accept from within will become a part of your outward experience. This is the secret and the miracle.

The Will of God for us is always better than anything we could think of for ourselves.

Do not "outline" how things are to come to pass. Claim your good and let the Great Power bring it forth into visibility.

You cannot do or have anything without the consciousness for it, so do not be concerned with appearances. Change your consciousness!

God is the only cause, but when we acknowledge any limitations we are limiting God and acknowledging a second cause.

Like attracts like. What you think in your mind will produce in your experience.

The only limitation that man has is the limitation that he sets for himself.

All the Power of the Universe is within you, and through this Power you can have anything on earth you desire.

Make a list of what you want in life, claim it as your own, visualize the experience of having the fulfillment of your desires, affirm that it is done, and give thanks. Then stand by for a miracle!

So we started making our lists. (I say "we" because my wife enthusiastically joined me in this exciting adventure.) Our desires included a move back to Houston, a more meaningful career opportunity for me, an income that would allow us to have extra money—we even named a specific annual salary. We also put a beautiful new home with a swimming pool on the list, along with a membership in a country club.

I guess from what I'm saying it would seem that our needs and desires centered mostly on material things, with a little social status thrown in for good measure. That's true, and the reason was because we realized that it wasn't wrong to want "things"—that we could have, do, and be anything as long as it didn't hurt anyone else.

Of course, I had prayed most of my life, but prayer had always been in the form of tryng to influence God to do something for me or someone else. In this new way of thinking I began to understand that God wasn't a Supreme Person who granted favors if you begged and pleaded hard and often enough. Rather, I started to conceive of Him as a Universal Power that flows through the mind of man and translates thoughts into form and experience—and that the Power can work *for* man only as It can work *through* him.

We worked on our desires daily, imagining what we wanted in every detail and affirming that all the good we desired was now coming into visability. Within two months, things started happening.

First, the president of a large advertising and public relations firm in Houston wrote me about a position in his organization. I did not know this man, had never heard of him, and had not communicated with him in any way. I called him after receiving the letter, then flew to Houston for a meeting. The next month I was offered the job—at the exact salary that I had written on the list. We moved back to Houston three months later and were able to buy a lovely new home, very similar to the one imagined. Within a short time, we put in a swimming pool, the company paid for a membership in a country club for me, and just about everything on our desire list had come to pass—including a vice presidency and ownership in the company.

Why not spread the word and share the discovery?

The idea for this book first came to mind during the summer of 1968. We were demonstrating so much good in our lives that I just had to tell everyone, not just about myself, but about others on the Path—and a book seemed to be the logical avenue of expression. So the intensive research program began . . . reading, studying, investigating, examining case histories, talking to everyone who would listen, and asking questions about "people with the Power."

As I said, I had to tell everyone about my accomplishments, and I remember one individual who was obviously many levels above me in terms of consciousness advising me to be careful. He said, "When you make the initial contact with the inner Realm, you have available only the amount of creative energy that has been stored as a reserve in your deeper mind. When you tap that energy, it proceeds to work wonders in your life, but at some point in time the energy will be depleted and you will once again be functioning on your own limited human resources. You see, you are still relying on mental work, rather than hooking up with the Dynamo within. Consciously and to a degree, subconsciously, you know that there is a power at work in and through you, but at this point, there is a power *and* there is your mind. They are not yet as one; the concept has not been embodied as an individual identity."

I didn't listen.

The research continued, and by the early part of 1969 I had heard about what I now call "Superbeings"—people who have dominion over all outer experiences. They were also called the Enlightened Ones, Masters, Divine Lights, and Superminds, and it was claimed that they do occupy earth space now and are continually growing in number. I was also told that the concept of Superbeings was not new—that according to ancient Jewish lore, there are a group of "Zaddikim" in every generation, believed to number at least 36, whose power is complete over mind and matter.

I was then led to a number of individuals in higher levels of consciousness. We heard personal testimony of the Infinite Power at work from a psychotherapist, an author, a psychic researcher, a scientist, the president of an insurance company, a movie star, a doctor, a magazine editor, Unity ministers, students of Science of Mind, and many, many others who are breaking out of the illusion of mortal mind.

The more I learned about the experiences and consciousness development of others, the more audacious I thought it would be to write a book about Superbeings while I was still outpicturing a very human consciousness with only a few demonstrations to talk about. After all, how could I tell you how to reach your maximum potential unless I had traveled the path before you?

So I decided to accelerate the research and study program and implant the Grand Design for a new consciousness. But in my haste I neglected the principles and short-circuited the whole process. In essence, I was given Aladdin's Lamp by the advanced souls and was told to handle it with care—and to read the instructions carefully. I didn't. I thought I knew enough to just rub the thing and my wishes would be granted. But the fine print said that if you rubbed it the wrong way it would blow up in your face. I saw that later, after I had put the pieces back together. You just can't play around with the one Great Power of the Universe. But I'm getting ahead of myself, so let's go back to September 1969.

It was then that I decided to "go for it"—to prove the principle and to do it in a way that would show. (Perhaps I wasn't thinking these precise thoughts at the time, but in retrospect, I see that my actions reflected this kind of thinking.) I set my sights on an annual salary exceeding $100,000 per year, the opportunity to have my own company, and all the trappings that would go with a rich and successful lifestyle.

In less than five months after beginning work on the new Mind Model, a man called me suggesting that I form my own company with his backing. I would be president and chief executive officer. Of course I accepted.

At the end of our first year in business, my new company had a profit of over a quarter-million dollars, and my personal income was well over $100,000. With this new prosperity I made several "sure-fire" investments, purchased two luxury automobiles, a magnificent home with over five thousand feet of living space on several acres—complete with a swimming pool. We entertained graciously, vacationed in the Carribean, and led the good life.

Then over the next few years, everything that I had built—quite obviously on sand—started crumbling. A business venture I was involved in collapsed, a man to whom I loaned money left the country, a merger with another company didn't work out, a client with a substantial bill offered to pay only 30 cents on the dollar, another with a large outstanding balance went out of business, and eight checks from a business associate bounced.

What had happened? I directed the question to a highly evolved soul—a true Superbeing. He responded by saying that the problem boiled down to the "phenomena of overextension"—caused probably by "ambition and enthusiasm untempered by adequate analysis."

Now that kind of rarified thinking is fine for Superbeings, but I needed something that worked—and fast. I wanted a miracle!

He went on to say that "a rubber check is an unkept promise. Had you been conscious of other unkept promises—either promises made to you or by you—either in your personal or business affairs? Or perhaps unkept promises which do not involve you personally or businesswise at all, but which aroused in you some sense of injustice or irritation? And might there be in your subconscious a negative conviction that 'Divine Supply is somehow distorted and diverted by human folly'—in effect saying that human folly controls Divine Wisdom?

"You might find it useful and enlightening to get into a meditative state and in imagination go as Daniel into the Lion's Den, listen to them growl, and command them to be still and to comfort you and reinforce your soul's true mission. Just giving them the Christly command, "Peace, Be Still" repeatedly until you begin to feel that every lion in the den is a willing cooperator in the fulfillment of your quest for spiritual mastery.

"It seems that we must come to the realization, the sure and immovable conviction, that any experience of contraction is a gathering of power—power which will flow according to the clearest pictures that we hold in our mind. I would work with sweeping, definite, gentle, persistent denials of all terror, panic, lack or loss. I would rest in the abiding place in which it is an unshakable certainty that now every thought and everything needed is being given, that you are totally receptive to the clear message of Divine Mind, and that you proceed with utter fearlessness to accomplish that which the Indwelling Spirit guides you to accomplish."

It wasn't until later that I realized how important this man was in moving me back on the Path. For one thing, he inspired me to listen (". . . you are totally receptive to the clear message of Divine Mind . . .")—and a listening attitude can work wonders in your life. The key thought that came forth from within went something like this: "Claim your good. Imagine your good. Speak the word for your good. Then care not if your good ever comes to pass."

That seemed to be quite a contradiction at first. If I desired something with all my heart, I *did* care if the desire was fulfilled or not. But the *caring*, which is another word for worry and concern, was actually diverting the power flow. I was told to choose what I wanted, see it as an actuality, call it forth into visible form and experience—then not be concerned about the outcome, regardless of how desperate the need.

An attitude of non-resistance is not the easiest thing in the world to attain. It is a "letting go and letting God" approach that relies on His Will to make a divine adjustment in your life and affairs. Of course, God's Will for each one of us is unlimited prosperity, health, happiness, joy, peace—the Infinite All. But the adjustment will not be made in your life until you change the make-up of your consciousness. I know.

I found that His Power can work for you only as it works through you, and while this impersonal Force can be the ticket to freedom, it can also throw you into bondage before you know what's happened. That's not God's Will. That's your will, because you do the choosing by the tone and shape of your consciousness.

In my particular case, I learned (after the fact) that I had tried to apply the Super-Power to the material world without first establishing the proper consciousness for what I desired. This jammed the circuits, so to speak, and the surge had no place to go except through some old thought patterns of insufficiency, selfishness, impatience and uncertainty, which I thought were dead and buried. In a sense, these unconscious or semi-conscious patterns were stirred up and called back into action to serve as outlet points for the Energy flow. Otherwise, I am told, a psychic fuse would have blown.

You see, everything you have and do is strictly in accordance with your consciousness. Emmet Fox once said that the explanation of all your problems can be summed up in the one statement—*Life is a state of consciousness.* In my particular case, I thought that I had a finely tuned prosperity consciousness based on the demonstrations that I'd had before, but obviously, I had only scratched the surface. As I had been told, I was "relying on mental work, rather than hooking up with the Dynamo within."

I immediately began to work on my consciousness with more comprehensive ideas based on the dynamics of Truth, and the outer scene did change for the better. As within, so without, "As a man thinketh in his heart, so is he." But at one point in time I gave up this project completely, saying to myself that if I couldn't prove the principles in more spectacular fashion, I certainly was not qualified to try to tell others how to reach the high road to freedom.

And something within said, "What's *right* with you?"

That's the kind of question that makes you think—and so I did—about the real positives of my life. My marriage of more than twenty-five years has been absolutely fantastic, and the love, friendship and fun with our two daughters, Susan and Leslie, has been beautiful. We have also been blessed with several close friendships that grow even more meaningful with each passing year. I've been successful in my career, and my wife and I have enjoyed radiant health. I continued with the list, and when it was completed, I saw all the good things that I had really just taken for granted.

And my Self said, "You should acknowledge what is *right* with you everyday and the good will grow."

I responded, "Sometimes it is difficult to acknowledge the good when my mind still sees incompleteness and imperfection in many areas of my life."

My Self countered: "If you wait for perfection, the purpose of this book will not be fulfilled."

"What is its purpose?" I asked.

"To reveal the Truth that every man and woman on Earth is more than a human being, that each has the Gift and may rise above all limitations of mind, body and affairs. As the fulfillment you are seeking is found by rising in consciousness, you will be demonstrating the Truth, and as you share these experiences with others, and as they share their experiences with you, you will grow together. You, and others who will join with you in the journey, are seeking the Fourth Dimensional Consciousness, which was established within all mankind in the beginning. It is in the depths of your being now, awaiting your rediscovery.

"Call your group *Quartus*.[1] It is not to be a church or a religion. It is to be a foundation for continued research and communications on the Reality and Truth of Man and his world. It is to be a platform for the free exchange of ideas, for opening minds, for sharing and growth. Now get on with the book."

And so *Quartus* was born. In the meantime, my life has taken many exciting turns, and while not all have been upward, every single experience has taught me something new about the state of my consciousness. And with every degree of change, I can see a corresponding effect in my world and affairs. I'm certainly not "home" yet, but I know that I've embarked on the most exciting and fulfilling journey of my life.

Care to join me? As we probe the mysteries within and touch the fountainhead of Power—and share our experiences with each other—we will grow together. And at a point in time, perhaps we will join the ranks of the true Superbeings—"the first faint beginnings of another race" on Planet Earth.

In Appreciation.

With the assistance of the Teachers, I have attempted to chart a course that we all can follow to this Super-realm within. In that regard, perhaps the title of this book should have been "How to be a Superbeing." That may have been more appropriate because much of the material has been devoted to ways and means of bringing our lives up to the level of our highest vision . . . so that

[1] The word *Quartus*, as defined in the Metaphysical Bible Dictionary, means a positive, spiritually enlightened thought that relates to the four-square (fourth) or perfectly rounded consciousness of the individual. *Quartus* bespeaks the elevating of the two phases of man, the head and the heart, understanding and affection, to the plane of spiritual wisdom and love, and the uniting of them in consciousness. *Quartus* suggests the bringing of the fourth dimension into man's comprehension. For additional information, please see the Appendix.

we may all become the true Superbeings that we were created to be.

I earnestly hope that in my personal interpretation of the wisdom and inspired thinking of these Advanced Souls, I did not lose the dynamic spirit of their message. Also, the printed word cannot capture or convey the life, love and enthusiasm with which the message was given by Jason, Elana, Daniel, Patrick, and the others.

To each one, I express my deepest gratitude for the new Light on the Path.

John Randolph Price

CHAPTER ONE

The Awakening

The revolution has begun. It started more than one hundred years ago, but now the pace is quickening. Throughout the world, men and women are joining in the uprising (the rising up) and are coming forward to be counted as part of a new race that will someday rule the universe.

The rebellion is against lack, limitation, disease, loneliness, failure and unfulfillment. Being overthrown is the authority which says there is an avenging and withholding God who could possibly cause such sorrow and suffering. The great illusion that man is the victim and not the master is being shattered. Man is beginning to stir from his deep sleep; a few have already awakened and have taken their place in strategic points around the globe.

The evolution of man into his next stage of development has been fueled with a cosmic energy causing incredible acceleration—as if to meet a universal timetable for the ushering in of the New Age. Jesus' deep metaphysical teachings are now being understood more fully by millions of people seeking the Light, and science and religion are joining hands in a new joint venture into the exploration of a nonmaterial world composed of pure energy. The Kingdom, or the Reality of the Universe, is indeed being discovered as never before.

Dr. Donald Hatch Andrews, Professor Emeritus of Chemistry at Johns Hopkins University, has said—"It is not seeing with the eye but seeing with the mind that gives us a basis for belief, and in this way science and religion are one. We are now entering an age when we will hold the power of life in our hands, and if it is to be used properly it must be in a world dominated by love. What we must have in the world today is a chain reaction of the human spirit. If we can feel this vision and if we can act on it, if we can transmit this vision to others and persuade everyone that living in terms of the spirit is the only answer, then we can change the face of the world."

And the face of the world *is* changing. The Great Awakening *is* taking place. In the cities and towns across America, hardly a week goes by without a symposium, seminar or workshop on spiritual healing, extrasensory perception, the survival of man, love and the meaning of human relationships, overcoming fear, new age living, the power within, creative imagination, the dynamics of positive thinking, mind control, awareness training, higher sense perception, the art of meditation, new dimensions of consciousness, holistic medicine, yoga, the inner meaning of life, and success and achievement.

Mental Science Institutes are involved in biofeedback research . . . corporations in the U. S. and abroad are developing new safety programs based on employees' biorhythm cycles . . . the American Management Association is publishing books on meditation for business people . . . Gallup Polls show that the majority of Americans believe in paranormal phenomena . . . books on the human potential are continually on the best seller lists . . . and Unity and Religious Science Churches are conducting services to overflowing crowds.

As a modern prophet once said, "*The world is going metaphysical.*"

This is not by chance. According to one Advanced Soul interviewed in this book, "Through the silent, hidden work of the Masters, men and women throughout the world are beginning to intuitively understand the Truth. There is a vibration, call it the Master Vibration, that is flowing through the consciousness of mankind, turning each individual toward the Light within, and it is only a matter of time before the Dawning."

The Masters—or what we call the higher ranking Superbeings—have pushed through the barriers of humanhood and are the first of a new species of mankind. They are the Leaders, the Teachers, and their work is being accomplished through the great medium of mind. Since all mankind is one and interrelated on the subjective level, these Earth Masters are releasing powerful waves of thought energy into this universal consciousness for the benefit and upliftment of each individual. To those who are receptive, the message is clear: "Rise up out of the tomb of mortality and take your place among the Enlightened of this world. Look up and see the unreality of sickness and poverty. Step out into the Kingdom of wholeness and abundance, peace and joy. The time is near for the New Age to begin."

These highly evolved Souls are helping us to break the hypnotic spell that has paralyzed us with fear . . . the fear of dying, the fear of disease, the fear of lack, the fear of loneliness, the fear of (add your own pet anxiety). They are revealing to us that we are immortal, potentially perfect in mind and body, abundantly supplied with everything needed, with the capacity to love and be loved that is beyond our present imagination.

If you cannot accept this, it is because you are thinking of yourself as "only human"—and you believe that every experience must reflect your humanhood.

You are not alone in this way of thinking. For many of us, anything out of the ordinary and bordering on the Supernormal is dismissed as science (or religious) fiction—not real, as if we really knew the meaning of reality. There may be an intellectual curiosity concerning instant healings, sudden prosperity, new found success, and other unaccountable experiences of people we know or hear about, but if it doesn't directly and intimately affect us, it's quickly put out of mind so that we can get on with the business at hand.

Then when our mirror of life begins to crack, we start looking for answers—and "What's the meaning of it all?" becomes the question. We intuitively know that there is more to life than we have been experiencing, but the treadmill runs in circles and we don't know when, where or how to get off. And while we are spinning in our own self-doubt, confusion and frustration, we may become aware of others who lead carefree lives, poised, confident, loved and loving, abundantly prospered, highly successful in their chosen careers, radiantly healthy, never at a loss for anything. Maybe they don't read minds or levitate—but there's something about them that makes them different. They *flow* through life, rather than plod or struggle, and if a problem comes their way, it suddenly disappears before it affects them.

These individuals must be considered a part of the new race of Superbeings. They did not suddenly "arrive" at this uplifted state of consciousness. It evolved over a period of time, and with each step forward their intunement with the power became more pronounced. Finally, they reached the stage of Harmony, where the body is maintained in proper balance, financial affairs reflect greater abundance, and fulfillment is the order of the day. But not content with just the "good" of this world, they pressed on—and depending on their vision—many reached the higher phases of evolution and are calling for others to join their ranks. They are inviting *you* to move up to the level of mastery, but they understand that you must first be freed of the fears, cares and concerns of daily living—so they ask you to choose what will bring you joy and peace at this time in your life. For example . . .

If you're lonely, you'll choose companionship . . . the right person to share your life and love, plus a multitude of caring and sharing friends.

If you're having financial problems, you will choose an immediate solution—with an abundance of money continuing to flow in so that all financial insecurities are a thing of the past.

If you're ill, you'll choose to get well and to maintain perfect health.

If you're unhappy with your job, you'll choose your "true place"—where total fulfillment is an everyday occurence in your life's work.

If you're tied up in entanglements and difficulties, you'll choose to be cut free and set on the highroad of freedom.

If you're uncertain and indecisive, you'll choose guidance.

If there is a broken relationship, you'll choose to have it healed for the good of all concerned.

You see, the advanced Superbeings know that we will not be ready in consciousness to take our place in the

New World unless we are well—well spiritually, mentally, emotionally, physically, and financially. So their objective is to turn us within, toward the Light, toward the Superconsciousness within each one of us where all the good we could possibly conceive is waiting to be released.

But *you* must make the choice. You must make the decision to live for the pure joy of it . . . to literally experience the Kingdom on earth NOW! And you can—because you have the Power to achieve your heart's desires.

The Power

There is a Power within you that is responsive to your needs. When you make conscious contact with this Power, it will literally transform your life because in your true nature, you are this Power in expression. You are in truth a potential *Superbeing.*

What is this Power? Where did it come from and what is its purpose? To find the answer we must go back to the beginning. In the beginning, Infinite Love, Power, Wisdom and Life—and all that we know God to be—created Man in Its image and likeness. (When we say "Man" —we are talking about the Individual, whether male or female.) In other words, Infinite Being expressed Itself as an infinite number of distinct beings or units of consciousness.

Man is, in his true nature, an individualization of God. In scientific terms, man is a manifestation or offspring of the Universal Creative Energy. This means that *you* are the Self-expression of the Infinite Power of the Universe. Now think for a moment. Since you are the Self-expression of the Infinite Mind of the Universe, then the Whole of that Mind must be right where you are. The Presence that is eternally expressing *as* you cannot very well leave or forsake Its own Self-expression can

It? Do you understand what this means? It means that the Allness of God, the Living Spirit of Creation, is around, beside and within you, projecting Its infinite attributes *as* you. So you are not only the image and likeness of God, but you are forever one with your Source. And since your Source has no limitations, neither do you!

This message is found in numerous ancient works, all through the Bible, and in writings that appeared several hundred years after the time of Jesus. In the *Decline and Fall of the Roman Empire*, Gibbon reports that during the first century of Christianity, the lame walked, the blind saw, the sick were healed, the dead were raised, and the laws of nature frequently suspended.

The use of the Power continued. ". . . in the days of Irenasus, about the end of the second century, the resurrection of the dead was far from being esteemed an uncommon event . . ." And in Gibbon's reference to the suspension of the laws of nature, one of the most common occurrences was the phenomena of multiplication—similar to Christ's "miraculous" feeding of the multitudes. But food was not the only physical manifestation brought forth out of mind. Whatever needed was provided.

Perhaps what Plotinus wrote during the second century was reflected in man's consciousness at that time: "There is in all of us a higher man . . . a man more entirely of the celestial rank, almost a god, reproducing God. When the soul begins again to mount, it comes not to something alien but to its very self. The self thus lifted, we are in the likeness of the Supreme."

Isn't this what St. Augustine meant when he said, "I sought thee at a distance, and did not know that thou wast near. I sought thee abroad, and behold, Thou was within me."

However, because of the repression of the individual,

the awareness of an indwelling Presence rapidly faded, and except for an underground movement of thought, it was not until the early 1800's that the Truth Idea came out into the light again. Until that time, anyone disagreeing with the established church was tortured or beheaded. If you were not a "Christian" according to the definition spelled out by the authorities of the state religion, you were in serious trouble. Only when the (first) Age of Enlightenment arrived in the eighteenth century could an individual discuss his or her inner feelings about the diety. Because of this repression, many who believed in the teachings of Jesus (which were truths brought forth from the ancient past) declared themselves non-Christian. They were not Christian from the standpoint of the state's interpretation, rather they were "Christed" according to the Truth revealed from within. They understood the brotherhood of man and the Fatherhood of God, whether the religion was Nature, Judaism, Buddhism, Islam, Christianity, or the old religion of White Magic. But this kind of thinking was considered pagan worship, and so it was either go underground or be punished or killed for your beliefs.

Finally, the consciousness of the race mind evolved to the point of partial enlightenment, and the true religionists of this planet emerged. Ralph Waldo Emerson has been called the modern prophet of the Truth revival . . . "Jesus Christ saw that God incarnates himself in man, and evermore goes forth anew to take possession of his world" . . . "What we commonly call man, the eating, drinking, planting, counting man, does not, as we know him, represent himself, but misrepresents himself" . . . "by unlocking at all risks his human doors, (man) is caught up into the life of the universe, his speech is thunder, his thought is law . . ."

Emerson was the prophet, but the rediscovery of Truth from the standpoint of its practical application in daily life has been attributed to Phineas Park Quimby, a clock-maker who lived in Portland, Maine in the nineteenth century. From Quinby's demonstrations of the Power at work, the word quickly spread—and as if a mystical curtain had parted—men and women with Supermind powers appeared throughout the world to teach the Truth of Being . . . that the "I" of you is the Self-expression of the Infinite Power of the Universe . . . that the Source or Cause of this expression cannot know or endorse anything but perfect harmony in each individual life. In the minds of all who were receptive to the teaching, the stern, condemning, dictator-God fell from the sky along with his big black book listing our sins and shortcomings. The man-made god was dead, and in its place was the Universal Reality of Love that had been present with us, in us, and *as* us from the beginning.

The fruits of this teaching have filled hundreds of books in the past century, but the documented reports covered more than levitation, telepathy, and other psychic phenomena. Rather, there was testimony to incredible healings, miraculous demonstrations of prosperity, the harmonious mending of broken relationships, the fulfillment of love and companionship, and the attainment of true-place career success.

The proof was in: *The principle could not fail.*

The Seeding of the Race Consciousness

One Advanced Soul who has been very helpful in the preparation of this book was questioned about the number of Superbeings involved in worldwide work, and the nature of their activities. His response was that there are several hundred Earth Masters at work in various points around the globe, but no number was given regarding the Universal Masters. (The levels of Master Consciousness are discussed in a subsequent chapter.)

It was also estimated that more than 50-million indi-

9

viduals were on this planet now operating from a predominantly spiritual or Christ consciousness—with at least half-a-billion men and women actively and purposely seeking new dimensions in consciousness.

The more evolved souls—the true Superbeings—are concentrating on a wide range of activities including writing, public speaking, individual counseling, special prayer work, meditation, and periods in the Silence. Not all are metaphysical and religious leaders, however. There are physicists, psychologists, family doctors, college professors, neurosurgeons, biologists, statesmen, business leaders, entertainers, housewives, and many others who are contributing to a New World Consciousness.

Their major objective is the upliftment of consciousness on a global scale, which includes the changing of certain erroneous beliefs in the race mind—the collective consciousness of mankind. The ideas (seeds) that are being planted in this mental atmosphere include . . .

All there is is God . . . the one presence and power of the universe . . . all loving, all wise, all knowing, all powerful. Every visible thing is an expression of God . . . all is God in different degrees of manifestation.

The realization that *all is God* has dispelled fear, assured protection, eradicated disease, and brought forth peace and harmony. This understanding has saved crops, averted an airplane disaster, and in one case in particular, helped a woman rise above a fear complex that had dominated her life for more than twenty years.

Lorna C. had grown up in a home permeated with an atmosphere of fear. Her mother constantly told her of the dangers of life and so overly-protected her that Lorna withdrew into a shell to avoid the terrors of the world. Even the simple act of walking home from school caused great apprehension, and dating conjured up so many threatening images that she fled from all possible relationships with the opposite sex. For years she hid in a darkened room in consciousness, suffering from a variety of physical ailments and living a life of very quiet desperation.

Then one day someone gave her a copy of *Lessons in Truth*[1] by H. Emilie Cady, and in the fifth chapter she found this statement: "God is Omnipresence (everywhere present), and God is good. Then why fear evil? He is Omnipotence (all-powerful). Then what other power can prevail?"

Lorna read this thought over and over again. She memorized it, contemplated it, and meditated on the meaning of the message. Slowly this truth penetrated into her subconscious mind and her fears gradually began to sink into nothingness. She began to read other books of a metaphysical nature, and with great dedication entered into a program of daily prayer and meditation. Within a year, she was literally not the same person. Former acquaintances were astounded by her outgoing personality, her sense of well-being, and her approaching marriage to a prominant attorney. In essence, she had become herSelf.

Another idea being sown by those on the Path is . . .

Man is the highest manifestation of God. Man is God in expression, the image and likeness of God, the very spirit of God individualized.

Every man in his true nature is the Christ, a son of God—just like Jesus. The difference in every man and Jesus is that He totally realized His Identity and relation-

---

[1] *Lessons in Truth*, H. Emilie Cady, published by Unity Books, Unity Village, Mo.

ship to God and we have not as yet. Man can unite his consciousness with the Consciousness of God, for they are one, and bring forth the Supermind—as in the case of George S.

George heard at an early age that he and all men were "worms of the dust"—fallen from grace—and destined to plod through life as a miserable sinner. His dull, drab life reflected this belief. His career as a school teacher was less than mediocre, and his personality could best be described as "colorless." But a new expansion of consciousness began one evening while George was attending a prosperity seminar. Today, he is one of the nation's most successful insurance salesmen and is a frequent speaker at success and motivation seminars.

When George was asked what he remembered most about that magic evening five years ago, he said—"I was introduced to my Self, and for the first time in my life I understood, I mean *really understood*, that God was my Father and I was His child. The significance of this was almost mind-boggling. As a son of God I was heir to His Kingdom, and I learned that I could stake my claim to my share of the Kingdom right here and now in this lifetime. Obviously, my Self-image changed dramatically that night."

A Truth idea that may have helped George was . . .

The idea of "original sin" is totally false. That a God of love and infinite wisdom would tempt man is absurd—and is not in keeping with the nature of God. The High Religion has nothing to do with sin, only the spiritual development of man.

Another idea that has changed many lives is . . .

Each individual is a special, unique individualization of God with the power of choice. Therefore, we create our own world with our minds. Thought is creative; thinking controls all action. The Law of Being says that consciousness must outpicture itself.

When a man or woman realizes that mind is the shaper and molder of events, circumstances and experiences, the process of achieving mastery begins. As the owner of a successful chain of retail stores states: "I rule my world from the laboratory of my mind and all action follows. My consciousness is the cause, and what happens around me and to me is the effect of my own thinking. God never punishes us, for He withholds no good thing. We punish ourselves by reaping what we sow, according to the law of cause and effect."

Other Truth ideas that are growing in the race mind include . . .

Man is God-Life in expression, and this Life cannot contain disease. God is our perfect health, and as we realize this Truth, it will be reflected in our bodies.

The abundant life for each individual is the Will of God. God is the source of all prosperity and is forever providing us with whatever we need in abundant measure.

Meditation is the way of entering the inner Kingdom, and can be a dynamic life-changing experience.

Man is immortal and has eternal life. There is no death— simply a passing from one plane of life to another.

Reincarnation is an absolute certainty.

No religious authority should ever stand between man and his consciousness of God. The voice of God within speaks directly to each individual.

Evil exists only in our minds—it is a human creation, which Jesus told us not to resist. When we achieve a con-

sciousness of Truth, evil disappears in our lives. It is not real, but can "appear" real if we fight it.

"The inspired, infallible Word of God" is the Christ indwelling each individual. The Bible was not intended to be interpreted literally in all its parts. It must be read through the heart and interpreted through the spirit.

Of course, these ideas are only samplings of the dynamic living Truth that is constantly being poured into the stream of race consciousness for the upliftment of all mankind. And by knowing the Truth, man is finding the freedom that is his divine birthright . . . freedom from fear, failure, futility, disease, poverty, tangled relationships, and all of the other maladies of "humanhood."

Mankind is indeed moving toward the Light as never before. The Awakening has begun!

CHAPTER TWO

The
Superconsciousness

When our search for the Superbeings first began, we solicited the views and assistance of many of the leading figures in the metaphysical field. We said in part . . . "there are *Superbeings* on this earth now, men and women who have realized their true identity to such an extent that they are no longer bound by the ills, limitations and problems of this world.

"I am not suggesting that the divine incarnation is so complete that these people approach the consciousness of Jesus. However, I feel that certain individuals have advanced to the point of achieving mastery in this earth life. Do you agree? Are there individuals today who have tapped and are continuously using the supermind realms? Are there those who have comprehended the secrets of mind so completely that nothing is impossible to them?"

Our inquiries prompted numerous letters, telephone calls and many stimulating conversations.

From a spiritual counselor in Georgia: "There has

been a tradition in many cultures for centuries of Avatars or fully illumined souls who have come into the world to assist in mankind's evolution."

A prominent metaphysical teacher in California agreed, saying that "regardless of what you call them, I am sure there are highly evolved souls who come forth on this earth plane at specific periods to do a specialized work of carrying forward the race in various ways. Some of these might work in the metaphysical field and be among its leaders, such as the Fillmores of Unity, Dr. Ernest Holmes of Religious Science, and Nona Brooks of Divine Science. Other highly evolved souls might come forth to work in the fields of science, medicine, aerospace, education, politics, to help carry forward the progress of the race in those fields. Others might function in still other ways, perhaps in what seems mundane areas, such as the home, to teach and provide assistance in various ways to those about them.

"Along with those who come forth already evolved, it seems to me that many people have this potential within them which they can bring out and use in this life experience, if they learn how to do so with the study of Truth, through the practice of meditation, affirmations, etc., thereby tapping the Supermind or Infinite Intelligence within them. Many people are in the process of doing this today through their spiritual and metaphysical studies.

One man—who referred to himself as simply a "student of Truth"—said "They (the Superbeings) are the truly happy people of this world. They recognize who and what they are, and with a knowledge of the universal laws, they are able to function as an open channel for the mighty currents that flow in and through man. They know that perfect health is their inheritance, and they demonstrate this truth. Rather than being a slave to money, they have reversed the process and have mastered the idea of an inexhaustible supply, and their needs are fulfilled. I cannot go so far as to say that nothing is impossible to them, but from what I've seen, a new species of man is coming forth to lead us out of the darkness and into a new dimension scarcely dreamed of by ninety percent of the people in this world. This will be the *New Age* of Enlightenment, and science and religion will join hands in spreading the truth that man is not the man we thought he was. I thank God that I live at this time and will be able to see the next great leap forward in man's expanding consciousness."

"I strongly evidence or identify with aspects of the Supermind in numerous individuals," said the president of a large metaphysical association. "I know the Supermind is within each individual. And the more I understand and develop my own infinite potential, the more I will become aware of this expressed potential in others, I am sure. What you are researching is valid, indeed. You will find what you are looking for. I personally feel that with what you are doing, with what others are doing, and with what each of us is becoming aware of, our present states of consciousness will appear as dreams in the next 15 to 20 years. This is how much I believe in the pureness, wholeness and intelligence of each potential Superbeing."

One researcher-author enthusiastically said, "They are everywhere. You will find them in every country, in every city. Hardly a day passes that a seemingly average human being suddenly awakens and finds that he or she is not the same person. It may have taken years of study and training to reach this point, or it may be that the time has come for this particular individual because of some special experience that releases the inner Light. But for whatever the reason, they rise up to take their place among the Enlightened of this world. And the very existence of this world depends on them.

"You will find your Superbeings. You would not be on this quest if the idea had not been planted in your mind. Perhaps your writings will help to bring people back into the realm of spiritual consciousness, which will be necessary if we are to eliminate poverty, disease, family conflict, failure, war, and all of the other maladies of man."

A delightful Superbeing, who also happens to be a minister in Houston, added this comment: "Truly, we live in an incredible age and we are just beginning to discover and hopefully rightly comprehend the mind of man. We are all powerful ideas in the mind of the Infinite and the time has come for us to do something more creative and adventurous about it."

The author of several metaphysical books suggested we review the book *Cosmic Consciousness* written by Dr. Richard M. Bucke. Dr. Bucke addressed the British Medical Association in 1894, telling the physicians in the audience that man's spiritual consciousness was becoming increasingly common—and that the development of the cosmic, or spiritual, phase of the mind would one day lift the whole of human life to a higher plane.

Understand that "spiritual consciousness" does not necessarily refer to man's religion, but rather to his awareness and understanding of his true identity. We all know people who are supposedly very "religious"—yet the life they experience on this earth may be more hell than heaven. And to blame any misfortune on God, as if it could possibly be His will, is total ignorance. God's will for man and all creation is absolute good, and He cannot will or endorse sickness or limitation of any kind.

To develop spiritually does not mean just going to church on Sunday and being "good" to appease an angry god who is keeping score somewhere in the sky. *There is no such god!* To grow spiritually means the increase of one's understanding of the true nature of God, man, and the creative laws of the universe.

When Dr. Bucke predicted the spiritual evolution of mankind, he was talking about the development of a new kind of consciousness, far in advance of the human self as we know it . . . the kind of consciousness that would eventually free the human race from sickness, poverty, ignorance, and above all else—fear.

You may be thinking that with the world situation the way it is now, all the Superbeings on earth must be in hiding. Not true. In spite of economic conditions, unemployment, the increasing crime rate, accident statistics, disease, poverty, and the threat of conflict, a Power is at work in this world that will be of undreamed of benefit to the whole human race.

When?

As one Truth teacher told me, "There is a distinct correlation between the inner and outer world." In other words, what is going on in the minds of the evolved and evolving souls on this planet will be manifested in the outer world of form and experience. "However," as the teacher put it, "the correlation is not always exact on the time scale, insofar as our limited awareness is concerned."

We must understand that while an increasing number of people are doing their part to change the race consciousness and bring forth the good that is the rightful possession of all, the great majority of people are continuing to use their minds in a negative and fearful way. But like running fresh water into a muddy glass, the water will eventually begin to clear as the mud is washed out. We will agree that there is quite an accumulation of muck in the combined thinking of the human race, but the pure water of Truth pouring forth from the Superconsciousness within each of us, and from the Superminds who are working daily throughout the world, will one day clear the consciousness of mankind. And the door to the New Age will open.

The Twelve Phases

If every student of Truth wore an identification tag, you would be amazed at the number and variety of people on the Path. The actor and actress you enjoyed on television last evening, the man sitting beside you at the lunch counter, the woman you passed on the street, an educator, a banker, a congressman, the owner of a retail store, a business executive, an insurance man, an attorney, a doctor, a psychologist, a scientist, a minister, a realtor, the salesman who called on you yesterday, the mother with the two children you saw in the supermarket . . . there is a good possibility that a man or woman you know by name may even be an Illumined One—a true Superbeing. They come from all walks of life and their number is growing daily.

I have found that people usually fall into several categories of consciousness, evolving from what is considered "Phase One" up to "Phase Twelve"—where the individual has so merged with the Power that you cannot tell one from the other. In describing these various phases I have covered only the basic characteristics of each level. I should mention that an individual may tap into the Power during his various stages and encounter experiences far above the norm for his present evolvement—such as a *Phase Seven* materializing form out of the ethers, an individual in *Phase Three* speaking the word for a healing in a highly critical situation, or a *Phase One* person experiencing psychic phenomena.

But even though there may be a temporary breakthrough into other elevations, for the most part the individual will remain in his or her state of consciousness until there is a "stirring within" to come up higher. This may come about as a result of a desperate need, or simply because the time is right. However, it is not until the Sixth Level has been attained that a person can be considered a true *Superbeing*—based on our current knowledge of the evolution of consciousness.

Phase One

A *Phase One* person may or may not have an awareness of his true identity—and if he does, it is only an assumption; there is no comprehension of the real meaning of this revelation. However, a person in this category may have a strong self-image as a human being, and even though his overall belief system may be faulty, he can on occasion "pull himself up by his bootstraps" and overcome handicaps and achieve a degree of success through sheer sweat, strain and personal will power. At the present time, the majority of people are in a *Phase One* consciousness—regardless of how "religious" they may profess to be.

Phase Two

In *Phase Two*, the understanding faculty is beginning to develop on an intellectual level. You perceive and approve of the idea that there is a Power within you, another Self on a higher vibrational level, a pattern of Perfection that is the potential You, a Higher Nature that can be brought forth into expression. It is all still a theory at this stage, but there is much enthusiasm for reading, studying and exploring of new ideas. There is interest in the techniques of self-actualization, mind dynamics, meditation, visualization and affirmations. Your mind is beginning to open and you are fascinated by your new discoveries.

Phase Three

The *Phase Three* person begins to feel subjectively that "Man's not all included between his hat and his boots" as

Walt Whitman put it. But the primary emphasis is on what can be done with "mind power"—basically a mental approach with little superconscious or spiritual foundation. The individual on the third rung usually tries to give the impression of being a bit mystical—the "I know something you don't" attitude, resulting in an exaggerated ego and much false pride. And when a *Phase Three* man or woman demonstrates a particular good, heaven help everyone within shouting distance because the experience is going to be told over and over again. If you can identify with this level, you know that you spend too much time trying to convert others to your "new" way of thinking with philosophical jargon that does nothing but turn people away. And you are retarding your own progress in the process. The key to moving past this stage is to keep your lips sealed and let the Power grow and develop.

Phase Four

The *Fourth Phase* must be entered into with great caution, because it is in this stage of consciousness that most Superbeings-in-training experience the greatest difficulty. In *Phase Four*, the Truth or spiritual faculty has been partially developed in your deeper mind, but is not ready for full expression. But because the consciousness tunes in at times to this illumined awareness, so-called miracles will occur, and there will be opportunities for magnificent demonstrations of the Power at work. At the same time, you may also find that your optimism is ahead of your understanding and errors in judgment will result, plunging you into a "how could this possibly happen" state of mind. It is not until the Truth Idea is fully manifest in consciousness that "miracle follows miracle and wonders never cease."

Phase Five

In *Phase Five*, an individual's consciousness is directed toward the good at least fifty-one percent of the time, i.e. the positive thoughts and feelings outweigh the negative. Now the clouds seem to part and more sunshine than ever comes into your life. There is more harmony, money is more plentiful, those old aches and pains are not as frequent, and things seem to be "right" in your life. The exceptional heights of sudden miracles and the deep valleys of futility experienced in Phase Four have passed, and there is more stability and order in life. The marvels and wonders indeed continue, but they are now recognized as the natural outpicturing of an uplifted consciousness rather than as supernormal. But there is a caution light on this level, too. People on the path say that Phase Five is straight and narrow, and if the shield of protection from the race mind is not strong enough to ward off concentrated negative influences, the scales of your mental atmosphere may be tipped and you'll find yourself backsliding into the roller coaster ride of Phase Four again. It is during the Fifth stage that a firm and definite commitment must be made, a covenant with your Higher Self, an unwavering dedication to principle. In essence, you now take your vows to achieve mastery.

Phase Six

Phase Six is the beginning of mastery, a dying to the old consciousness and a rebirth into a new understanding of the cosmic power within. This consciousness knows only spiritual man, and is content to simply experience this joyful communion. Very little outer work is done during this stage, and is thus referred to as the "sabbath" by the evolving souls. When you reach this level, you *know* you are the Power, but being a time of rest, the knowing is sufficient. By the Law of Consciousness, you experience harmony, but there is no strong desire to reach out and demonstrate your realization.

The next six phases, Seven through Twelve, signify the evolving consciousness culminating in total Mastery.

Phase Seven

As a Seven, you understand that you now have the power to establish a life of heaven on earth in this incarnation—and you begin to use the power accordingly. Creative imagination becomes a major factor in this stage and through it, you find the world shaping to your thoughts. You are quickly "placed" in work that is best suited for your talents and where you can experience the greatest fulfillment. There is financial security because you "see" all the money needed to achieve your purposes being attracted to you in abundant measure—and so it is. Your health is excellent, and your relationships with others loving and caring. The basic thinking of a Seven is to get his life up to the standard of his highest vision, and to achieve the maximum degree of livingness. And while it sounds as though a Seven is completely self-oriented, it must be pointed out that this stage represents a greater degree of givingness than the others before it. Reason: A Seven knows that he cannot use the power for himself without decreeing the same good for all others within the range of his consciousness and beyond. So as he sees himself as whole and complete, he sees everyone else according to the same divine standard. This is "loving thy neighbor as thyself."

Phase Eight

In *Phase Eight*, you know that your life is now in a more advanced stage—you are reaching wholeness in mind and body and your spiritual nature is in a higher degree of radiation. Your desires are fulfilled, so your attention begins to focus outwardly almost exclusively, and as if "by chance" people are attracted to you for guidance and counseling. In this phase you have remarkable healing powers for another's body and affairs, but your effectiveness depends to a great extent on the receptivity of the individual being treated. For that reason, you usually will not attract those who knew you when you were living out of a lower-vibration consciousness. It is during this stage that you will find a new light on the ancient Truth teachings. This Gift of wisdom and understanding will enable you to develop a new way of thinking and teaching based on the *extension* of this sacred body of Knowledge, and you will spend much time absorbing these new concepts and preparing the "message" for the people of the world.

Phase Nine

A *Phase Nine* person tends to "go public" with his Message. Here, your tendency is to attract a following for your particular teaching and miracle works. Where an Eight is more individual oriented, the Nine Man is committed to service on a much broader scale. The founders of Unity, Religious Science, The Infinite Way, and other New Thought groups were most likely men and women in this state of consciousness, along with many other spiritual teachers and writers of the past and present who are making significant contributions to the uplifting of the race mind.

Phase Ten

An individual in *Phase Ten* is an Earth Master, with dominion over matter and the forces of nature. He has the ability to project his spirit body and be seen at two places at the 'same time, and clairvoyance, clairaudience, telepathy and precognition are a part of his nature. Translating pure energy into visible form is another characteristic of a Ten. But it is interesting that as a soul passes from Phase Nine to Ten, he begins to separate himself from the masses and goes apart for a more solitary life of meditation and contemplation. Even so, the Power of a Ten radiates throughout the earth plane, enveloping the world with a light of an illumined consciousness. Others on the path frequently "tune in" to the consciousness of a Ten, with spectacular changes occuring in mind, body and affairs. Thus the evolution through the various phases is helped considerably by these Earth Masters.

Phase Eleven

Phase Eleven is the stage for Universal work, not only on earth but in other dimensions as well. A Master in this stage of evolution is able to move from the earth plane to the realms beyond and return at will. While a Master Ten is concerned primarily with earth life, the Master Eleven is more universal in scope, working on both sides of the "curtain"—helping in the evolution of all souls. The Masters frequently referred to in occult literature and in the ancient writings are in this stage of soul development.

Phase Twelve

A Soul in Phase Twelve is a Master of Heaven and Earth, and as far as we know, the last Twelve on Planet Earth was Jesus Christ. More about this Master Superbeing later.

The great majority of the advanced trainees and the Superbeings themselves (Phases Six through Nine)—are living lives that appear to be ordinary from all appearances. They raise families, pursue meaningful careers, watch television, enjoy vacations, engage in social activities, and participate in civic and community affairs. But the more advanced they are, the less they talk about their abilities—so you can enjoy a friendship with one and possibly not reaize that he or she is actively working with the Power in this life experience. But don't be too curious about that strange neighbor down the street, or the friend who seems to suddenly have it all together. Even with a close watch, you probably won't see either one practicing psychic tricks or flying around the backyard. The only truly recognizable feature of an advanced soul is the feeling *you* pick up when you are around one. Intuitively you know that you are in the presence of a higher consciousness; you sense a love vibration, a deep sense of peace, a radiance not usually expressed by ordinary mortals.

Just be content to know that in every community you will find individuals who are daily tapping the Super-mind and releasing a healing, prospering, guiding, protecting Power that does not understand the meaning of the word impossible. These men and women are not running around playing God. They *are* God—in expression, and they know that the human or earthly side of their nature is but a channel through which the Power works.

We are all on the Path—whether we know it or not

Even if a person has not developed the Supermind Consciousness yet, we must remember that there is that Something within every individual that is a motivating, uplifting force—whether or not the person is involved in consciousness training of a metaphysical nature. We all know scores of people who have not purposely charted a course leading to soul mastery, yet their lives reflect certain super-human characteristics that are brought into play when there is a need. They may have come into this world with a firmer consciousness in a particular area, or perhaps greater tenacity was developed through suffering and hardship, or their faith in God—regardless of what their comprehension of God may be—opened the windows of their souls if only for a moment. In that split second was a flash of Light, and the very Spirit of God "made all things new."

Whether we are Baptist, Catholic, Buddhist or Jew, we all have an inner Companion, and He is constantly trying to help us achieve all that we can conceive and believe—even when we are not aware of His presence.

I have a friend with a prosperity consciousness that many Superbeings-in-training would love to duplicate. He has the Midas touch and his ability to make money in abundant measure has been demonstrated in two separate professional careers and numerous sideline ventures. Whether he realizes it or not, he has accepted the Truth that prosperity is his birthright—as it is for all mankind. He subjectively knows that the only limitations man has are the limitations he places on himself, so there is absolutely no reason for him not to be wealthy. He has surrounded his "I" with an image of success, and without really understanding that this is the truth about him, he has developed a mind model of success and prosperity that reflects the Law of Abundance. It also helps that his wife has a highly developed intuitive sense, and I learned years ago the folly of not trusting her strong feelings about a particular situation.

Another couple whom I've known since college personify the attribute of *love* to such an extent that just being in their presence is an uplifting experience. They are caring, sharing people who love life and express the Christ nature of givingness to friends and strangers alike. This is the way we are all supposed to live, but we don't want to give up our self-centeredness and our self-righteousness. It is only when we have developed the spiritual quality of love, as this couple has, that life really begins to have meaning.

If love and joy are the attributes of a Superbeing, then my wife must be added to the list. I've shared my life with her for more than 28 years, and I think I've found her secret. She's really an angel masquerading as a human being. There's no other explanation. She radiates love and joy wherever she is, and for her each new day is a new experience to live, to feel, and to remember. It is true that she has helped me with the research for this book, and has been involved in the study of Truth—but this special uplifted consciousness has been evident since the first year of our marriage. Long before we ever heard of Superbeings, Jan told me that she was forming a club called the B.O.A.P.P. Society, and that she was going to be the charter memeber. She said there was only one requirement to join: You must believe you are the Best Of All Possible People—a BOAPP. "There's nothing conceited about this," she said. "It simply means that I like myself. That's important. There have been times when my membership lapsed because I didn't like myself very much—but most of my life my membership has been in good standing.

"I think everyone should join. It's healthy to like yourself. If you don't, you'll probably find a lot of things wrong with other people, too. So why not see the best in yourself, in others, and in the world?"

Later, when we both began to uncover some of the secrets of the Superbeings and the philosophy of the New Thought movement, she wrote: "What you believe becomes truth. It doesn't fail—ever. When I hold high thoughts about me and you, everything in my world blossoms. Low thoughts destroy.

"At first I didn't know how great I was . . . I really hadn't thought much about it. I guess I figured I was okay. But this man I married always thought I was better than I was and because I loved him so much I had to become what he believed. See how it works? Boapps create Boapps. You can't fake it. You must convince yourself and grow with it."

When we look for the divine in each individual, we usually find it—because all of us are so much more than we think we are.

Which reminds me of my mother. Time after time she has tapped the inner resources of divine strength to prove the perserverance of the human spirit. When the family drug store was lost during the Depression and my father became ill, she rolled up her sleeves and built her own business—evolving from a few meals served to roomers to one of the most successful family restaurants in Alice, Texas. And when my father died and the business burned down, she turned within again and emerged with new strength and courage to rebuild and achieve an even higher level of success. She later remarried and sold the business, but her talent for creating something from within came forth again—this time as an artist—and her paintings are now considered prized possessions by family and friends.

Someone once said that "perseverance and audacity generally win." And there's no doubt about it. Eva's a winner!

Do you understand what I'm driving at? Every single individual on the face of the earth and beyond has a divine attribute already in some degree of expression. And it is this spiritual "light" that we can use as our foundation on which to build a new and better life . . . the kind of life that is our divine heritage. This means that regardless of the level of our entry, we are all potential Superbeings *now*. We are all on the Path whether we know it or not, and if our Light is a prosperity consciousness, let's build on that and reach within to discover that this is only part of our true nature. If we have realized the divine quality of love, let's move on to discover all the secrets of the soul, knowing that love will open the portals faster than any other expression of the Living Christ within.

If strength is our link with spirit, then let us develop an even stronger spiritual basis for our life by knowing without a shadow of doubt that "I can do all things through Christ which strengtheneth me."

You must find *your* entry point to the upward path . . . you must determine which of the divine gifts is most pronounced in your consciouness and let it be the foundation on which to build a life that overcomes the world. It may be faith, or understanding, or imagination, or wisdom. Perhaps it's enthusiasm or good judgment. Whatever it is, it is your key to unlock the first door.

CHAPTER THREE

The Lesson

In my first encounter with Jason Andrews (not his real name), he handed me a piece of paper with "At-one-ment" written across the page. "This is the lesson," he said. Since that time we have had many talks, and this chapter is based on notes from several sessions with him.

"I was never born and will never die," said Jason. "I am immortal. It is impossible for me to suffer illness in any form, and I have never experienced any kind of an accident. I am as rich as any man who ever lived, I am totally successful in all my undertakings, I live a perfect life. I am continuously overflowing with love, joy and peace. Of course, this is the Truth about *all* people. What is true of one is true of all, when you consider the Reality of each individual. I am you and you are me and all is one. All is 'I'—I AM."

Jason settled back in the leather wing chair. "The most important thing to learn is that within every person, whether in this dimension or another, is a presence and a power—the same Presence and Power through which this universe was created. This Presence, this Mind, within each individual, is alive. It lives! It knows all. It *is* all.

"You could say that there are two of you sitting in that chair at this moment. An outer you and an inner You, an earth self and a Self who can never be bound by the limitations of earth life. I am not talking about the conscious and subconscious phases of your mind. I am talking about a living, thinking Spirit that functions on a deeper level, on a higher vibration. I am talking about the Reality of you, your God-Self, the universal Spirit of God contemplating Itself *as* you at the point where you are!

"This Presence within you, this God-Self of you, wants you to be radiantly healthy, because perfection is the true nature of Its expression. It wants you to be prosperous, because abundance is the nature of its manifestation. It wants you to be happy, at perfect peace, loving and loved, wise, successful, confident, enthusiastic, joyful, strong and free—because it is through these patterns of itself that it expresses Its true nature of wholeness, completeness and perfect harmony. You have the power within you at this very moment to realize the fulfillment of every desire. Through the love, wisdom and power of your indwelling Spirit, you have the ability to bring about any necessary change in your body or affairs."

He got up and walked to the window. After a few minutes of silence he continued. "Understand that there is only one Self in all the universe, one Selfhood, one infinite omnipresent Spirit—and everything in the manifest world is an idea in the mind of Spirit. This Spirit is thinking you and me and everyone else. You are a thought in Its Mind, and this thought is Its idea of Itself in expression. Can you see that nothing can be apart from God? Can you understand that nothing in all the world can be separated from God? The Spirit of God where you are—in and around and through you—is *your* Spirit. It is the one Presence and It is your Presence. Spirit is the absolute Reality of you. The Spirit where you are is contemplating Itself *as* you. It is thinking of Itself *as* you.

"This idea of you, this image of you in the Mind of your Spirit comes forth into expression as you, as your consciousness. Mind in expression. Mind *as* expression. God *as* you. Your inner Selfhood appears as you. You are a manifestation of the Spirit of God.

"Now do you see why there cannot be God *and* you? The sun and the sunbeam can never be separate. 'I and the Father are one. All that the Father is, I am, and all that the Father has is mine'. I am God in expression. You are God in expression, and we can never be separate from our Source.

"Think of it! The Infinite Mind of Spirit right where you are—*within you*. All Love, Life, Beauty, Wisdom, Intelligence, Power, Joy, Total Completeness. And could the thoughts of this Mind be different than Its true nature? Could God be less than God? The sum total of those thoughts about you, this image of you, is the Word of God. 'In the beginning was the Word, and the Word was with God, and the Word was God. And the Word was made flesh'. The Word comes forth into expression as you, as me, as each individual, as an inner Knowingness, as Truth itself, as the manifest Christ, as your Superconsciousness.

"This is the true nature of your being, regardless of how you think and feel from the limited consciousness of your mortal mind. The Light of God Mind is shining now in the depths of your soul as the Perfect Pattern, as the true I AM, but it will be of no benefit to you until you recognize it and accept it. Only when you embody the Reality of You will the Light spread throughout the subconscious phase of your mind, dispelling the darkness and eliminating all false beliefs. Only as the error convictions are replaced by the Spirit of Truth will your whole being be filled with Light. Then you will have the mind that was also in Christ Jesus.

"Too difficult a task for mere humans? Then consider this. Although it may take many lifetimes to even approach the fullness of power demonstrated by Jesus, you can rise above the problems that beset humanity while in this present life—and what is true for one is true for all. Defining 'sin' as a separation from God, it is a sin to be sick, poor, lonely, unfulfilled. By reestablishing the connection, and realizing the Truth, you and all mankind can rise above the lack and limitations of body and affairs in this lifetime. It is the Father's good pleasure to give you the Kingdom *now*, but you must accept and then live out of that Kingdom as the Supermind you were created to be. The *when* is in direct relationship to your priorities in life. When you want to be a co-creator with the Spirit of God within you, and consent to follow His every instruction, you are halfway home. The remaining distance will be covered when you begin to live the Truth moment by moment, hour by hour, day by day."

What is the biggest obstacle in attaining a realization of Truth?

Andrews: "Mental laziness. Not caring enough. A contentment with things as they are, even if the things include poor health and financial insufficiency. You always follow your priorities. You do what you choose to do. If you want to develop your Superconsciousness, there is nothing to hold you back. But if there is not a burning desire to do so, there will always be an excuse to put it off. Isn't that strange? I tell a person that he can have a perfect body, financial abundance, the ideal mate or companion, complete protection, total fulfillment, great success, and he says—"well, that sounds good, but I just don't have time to get involved with that now'.

"Of course, people on the Path do have to come out from under the influences of race mind thoughts, the combined thinking of the human race, both conscious and subconscious. This polluted mass has just about everything in it, and if you are not constantly on guard, you can tune into a race mind belief and throw yourself completely out of the stream of Truth. Take sickness as an example. If people believed more in health than in sickness, they would maintain healthier bodies, but most individuals think that it is normal for the body to 'catch something', or 'come down' with something, or to be susceptible to something outside the body, or to grow old and decay and fall apart. This is sheer nonsense, but if you are around people who talk the language of sickness all the time, it may be difficult to protect yourself. The same thing holds true when there is constant talk of lack and limitation. A more advanced soul does not worry about these negative influences as much, but most people have to be very careful not to accept such ideas and incorporate them into consciousness."

How can you live in this world and not recognize sickness, poverty and all the other maladies of mankind?

Andrews: "You can be aware of the mafia without letting the idea that that word represents become a part of your consciousness. You can be understanding and have compassion for people in ill health without believing as they do. The key is to look past the appearances and center your thoughts on the Real Self of the individual. If Mary is down with the flu, you know that the Reality of her is not sick and cannot be sick, and so you silently acknowledge that fact. You don't insult her by telling her that she's not sick, or that she feels fine. You understand that she's listening to the sickness station playing in her mind, but that does not mean you have to listen to it, too. No—you listen to the Truth within *you*, realizing that the only way you can help Mary is to be *Yourself*. Then you become a healing influence for all those within the range of your consciousness, including Mary."

Wouldn't that give the impression to other people that you are a cold, selfish and inconsiderate person?

Andrews: "Remember that I said to be *Yourself*. Until you reach the point in consciousness where you are a literal expression of your Higher Self, you must think, speak and act according to the nature of that Self. At least as much as you can. That would mean a person who is loving, caring, considerate, joyful, filled with peace and totally positive. So even if you cannot accept another's illness or lack or failure, you do not judge them. You acknowledge the perfection of their inner Being, and treat the outer person as you would wish to be treated.

What about people who have advanced to the consciousness of achieving total mastery in this earth life?

Andrews: "When you talk about *total* mastery, you are referring to only a few hundred souls who are actively working on this plane at any particular time. But there are millions of men and women on earth now who are in an advanced state of humanhood and who are evolving and are experiencing fewer and fewer limitations in mind and body.

"The Masters, however, are here with a particular mission and that mission is to raise the level of consciousness of all mankind. In addition to these Earth Masters, there is the Brotherhood . . . highly evolved Ones who pass between the seen and unseen worlds at will, and have full access to the Akashic Records. They may be considered students of Melchizedek, a secret Brotherhood that taught the Law of the One before the man Jesus walked the earth. Melchizedek was the Christ of his age, and later appeared as Jesus. Today the Brotherhood, working directly with the consciousness that expressed as Jesus and with the Earth Masters is setting the stage so to speak, for a new uplifting of the race consciousness, an ushering in of the fullness of the Aquarian Age and a New Heaven on Earth."

When will this take place?

Andrews: "Understand this. This New Age *will be*. A new Heaven on Earth *will be*. Preparations are being made now, and out of chaos will come the beginning of peace on earth, a New Order for mankind. The time depends on the hearts of men. The consciousness of the race has within it every false belief and negative emotion recorded since the beginning of time, but because the race mind is common to all, a change in one man's thinking influences the whole. Through the silent, hidden work of the Masters, men and women throughout the world are beginning to intuitively understand the Truth. There is a vibration, call it the Master Vibration, that is flowing through the consciousness of mankind, turning each individual toward the Light within, and it is only a matter of time before the Dawning."

What did you mean when you said 'out of chaos' will come the beginning of peace on earth? Will there be another war?

Andrews: "Chaos is here now. Nuclear-arms race in the Middle East; conflicts in Lebanon, Ireland, El Salvador, Iran; deaths by cancer, heart attacks and other diseases; the epidemic of drugs and alcoholism; the slayings in Atlanta; the rising divorce rate; families living in quiet desperation because of financial problems; the destruction of the environment; rampaging crime. Shall I continue? John, there is a war *now* in the hearts of mankind, but out of this darkness will come the Light. It is only unfortunate that the Adam man of earth today must, *by choice*, undergo suffering to ready himself for the transformation."

Would you say that the majority of people on earth today are living out a predominately negative consciousness?

Andrews: "The majority of people are not evil, but neither are they on a spiritual vibration in consciousness. Most are neutral, living in their own small space and content to spend their lives in a restricted mind— thinking only of protecting and promoting the lower self while unknowingly feeding the race consciousness with negative thoughts and emotions. What you have, then, are people with downward thinking and others who have chosen to express their higher nature, but the majority are human, neither devils or gods in consciousness— caught up in the mortal plane of illusion. It is to this group that we say—'choose this day whom you will serve'. Mankind must choose the higher side of life if it is to hasten the New Age."

You're saying that we must forget the concerns for ourselves and work for the higher good of mankind in general?

Andrews: "The good of the whole must begin with the good of the *individual*. If each person could only understand that once on the Path, not only is another soul added to the cause of good for the benefit of all, but the man, the woman is lifted into a new dimension of living. It is not selfish to want to be healthier, wealthier and more fulfilled in life, because you help the world when you help yourself. The rich and healthy people on this planet do more for all of mankind than those who are poor and ill. Remember, we are all one, all waves in the same ocean, and one man's consciousness of abundance and well-being with its outer mainfestations releases more light into the race consciousness for the benefit of all. So start with yourself. Do not preach to others. Do not argue. Do not judge or condemn. Begin with yourself. *Know yourself.* By knowing the Truth about yourself, the Law will do more to uplift the consciousness of mankind than you could possibly do with personal persuasion."

What do you mean by the Law?

Andrews: "The action or activity of God—of your Higher Self. You are a center of consciousness through which the Power of God flows. When you turn within and touch the realm of Spirit, your outer mind becomes a channel for the Power. The Power is the Law. It is the action of God Mind. It is Substance. It is Light. It is Thought Energy—the very Thought Energy of your Higher Self. This Self is always thinking thoughts of perfection . . . perfect health, perfect order, the perfect solution to every problem, the perfect answer for every need. It sees abundance instead of lack, health instead of illness, life instead of death. It sees total fulfillment for you, as you, and this Perfect Pattern of fulfillment is manifest now as your true nature. You are the Self-expression of the Infinite. God has fulfilled Himself as you."

Then why don't all people live perfect lives?

Andrews: "These thought patterns of perfection are focused within you now as the Christ of you, in a Superconsciousness of Sonship, as the Spirit of Truth. But you must recognize and accept this Idea before it can become objectified in your world. Until you embody the Truth, this spiritual energy must flow through a consciousness of imperfection. Your consciousness is your free will. You are free to think and feel as you choose, but in doing so, you are conditioning the flow according to your own limited thoughts. In essence, the Law becomes your servant. Even though it will flow from the Christ Center on a mission of the highest Vision, it will change its purpose, objective and destination according to the tone of your consciousness. As it proceeds from the Kingdom within to bring forth abundant supply to fill a need, it may pass through a conviction that says 'there is no way that I will have sufficient money to pay that bill'—so the Unlimited becomes limited and it will move heaven and earth to make sure that there is an insufficiency of money for the need. Why? Because *you* ordered that particular state of affairs. The same holds true for health. In the Mind of your Higher Self is the perfect body idea and this idea of a perfect body is forever expressing itself, sending forth the perfect image into every cell and organ of your body. But again, the Creative Energy must flow through your consciousness, and if your mental atmosphere is charged with a belief in sickness, then the Law will attract sickness to you. Remember what Jesus said— 'As a man thinketh in his heart, so is he'. You are what you think."

I'm reminded of the often-quoted statement—"What the mind can conceive and believe, the mind can achieve." It sounds like a simple process.

Andrews: "It is, but it is not easy. Much effort and discipline are required in controlling the conscious mind, because it is this phase of mind that feeds the subconscious. The subjective realm is totally impersonal. It does not judge. It accepts what you think and believe is true and sets up a vibration that corresponds to that particular concept. That vibration is like a slide in a projector. When the light moves through the slide, the image is projected on the screen. When the energy flows through the field of vibration, the image is projected on the outer screen of life.

"Outline this:

1. You have a conscious phase of mind with which you make decisions. It is the 'chooser' in your mental world.

2. Your subsconsciousness is subjective to your conscious mind. It accepts what you think and believe and sets up a vibration for every conviction you have. The combined vibrations make up the total pitch of our soul consciousness.

3. You have a Superconsciousness, which is your spiritual nature, and the law, emanating from this consciousness of Truth, moves constantly through the vibration field of your mind. There it takes on your now-identity and reproduces this consciousness in your body and affairs.

"When your thoughts, beliefs and feelings are in tune with your Truth Center, there is a mind-of-one-vibration. That is the Supermind of man, where nothing is impossible."

Is that a literal statement—that nothing is really impossible? What about walking through walls, materialization and . . .

Andrews: "Forgive me for interrupting, but ah! Now should we talk about magicians, wizards and new dimensions into the cosmic wonderland? Shall I levitate while turning water into wine? No, nothing is impossible, but phenomena should not be considered an end in itself. Every 'miracle' since the beginning of time has been accomplished according to natural laws that are beyond the comprehension of the average person. A highly evolved soul, through thought projection, may materialize form, and such events have been witnessed and verified in our own time. The moving of physical objects by mind is very common today, and dematerializations and materializations of the body have been reported numerous times. A Supermind can also mentally arrange the electrons of matter into a similar pattern, permitting the body to pass through an apparently solid substance. Everything that Jesus did is being duplicated today, just as he said it would."

What about the raising of the dead?

Andrews: "Read your newspapers and magazines. Hardly a month goes by without a report of someone who died and returned to life, and these are people who are declared medically 'dead' by their doctors—absolutely no sign of life. One man was already at the funeral home before he 'rose from the dead'. In subsequent interviews all the people tell a similar story of having left the body, looking down and seeing themselves in human form, then passing over to the other side, or into another dimension, and they describe the transition in some detail. These individuals were brought back, some unwillingly, by an Advanced Soul, or by the Power, the Light, released from their own indwelling Christ. And the reason was because they had not completed their mission on earth. Or rather, the design, the purpose of the Higher Self through these particular incarnations was not complete. Of course, there is no death, only a movement from one plane of life to another."

Should we believe in reincarnation?

Andrews: "Believe it or not, it is a fact. It is mentioned in the Bible by Jeremiah, Malachi, Jesus, Paul, in addition to several references in Genesis and in the Book of Revelation. When mankind lost its spiritual awareness, it began a cycle of entering and leaving the three dimensional plane, devoting time to the soul's evolution on both sides of the curtain. Look at it this way. You are forever you. You will never be anyone else and you will live forever. *You are forever you.* You are a unique, special individualization of God, and your whole purpose for being is to be a vehicle, a channel, for the expression of your inner Self.

"For most people, the door to the inner Presence is closed. 'I stand at the door and knock' said the Christ through Jesus. Until that door is opened, each soul is in evolutionary training, and this is where the Law of Karma comes into play. Remember we are here for one purpose only, and that is to find our way back to the Father's house—to be the true Self-expression of the Infinite. If our soul is evolving, and more and more Light is entering our consciousness, we are said to be on the Path, and when we finish our mission in this lifetime and make the transition to the other side, our work and study with the Masters will be more fruitful. In our next incarnation, then, our life will be on a higher level with the journey filled with greater love, order and harmony.

"Conversely, the lower the consciousness and the slower the growth, the more that must be compensated for in the next cycle. A life filled with an outpouring of hate and bigotry must return to be the recipient of that state of mind—the master returning as slave, the oppressor to be the oppressed, the thief to be taken from, the murderer to experience the darkness of his deed. And the cycle continues, as cause and effect, until the soul begins its upward movement, transcends Karma, and enters the realm of grace. Then the soul's onward march is under the guidance and direction of the Christ within, the inner Self, and each incarnation is an advancing stage. Finally, when man fully awakens to the truth of himself and realizes his Oneness with God, it will not be necessary to walk again on the earth plane.

"But I want you to understand that you can transcend Karma and cancel out every mistake, with the slate wiped clean, right here now, in this lifetime. This does not mean that you will have overcome the tendency toward error, or that you will necessarily cease the cycle of incarnations, but it does mean you can be forgiven of all transgressions of the Law. How? By accepting the forgiveness of your indwelling Christ. The idea of Forgiveness is a part of your deeper Consciousness, and this idea of Forgiveness is forever expressing itself. Recognize that forgiveness is a part of the divine Gift. Accept it. Realize it and you can be free of the past. But in order to realize it, you must cease living strictly in your emotional nature. You must give up all hostility, mental turmoil, resentment, condemnation. You must forgive yourself and everyone else. You must clean up and clear out your consciousness before the pure energy of Forgiveness can be received and embodied.

There are many religions and forms of worship on earth today. Is one closer to Truth than the others?

Andrews: "Religion is man's understanding of God, and because of the unique differences in consciousness, there are many different concepts, but most have been helpful in soul growth. However, if the foundation is based on One Presence, One Infinite Love, One Power, One God, One Supreme Being, One Father, with each individual a spiritual manifestation of the One, and with the Oneness of God and man as the central theme, then you are approaching the High Religion taught by the Masters.

"It has been said that most of civilization's wars were motivated by religion. I take exception to that. Wars have been inspired by people. All the suffering on Planet Earth since the beginning of time as we know it has been caused directly and only by the mind of man. There is no such thing as a vengeful God. Our experiences are always the result of our thoughts.

"This is why you must be so careful not to fall under the spell of someone who is spreading *his* word as the Word of God. Even what I say, you must prove for yourself, and you must be *free* to do so. I will not dignify cults by even discussing them, except to say that any group that attempts to imprison the mind and stifle the spirit of man—whether in the name of love or scientific adventure—will eventually reap the destructiveness that it has sown.

"All of the world's *major* religions serve a purpose in the redeeming of the soul and leading mankind back to the single path to the mount, because all speak to a particular level of consciousness. Never condemn another's religion, because that particular teaching may be vitally important to his soul growth at that point in time. But prophets, teachers and preachers do emerge from time to time who would hinder the soul's growth with messages that contradict the nature of God, which is Love, and the nature of life, which is joy. Many speak via the avenue of mass media from the platform of organized religion and from the Bible, and so there is credibility to their words. But if they condemn and judge others, if they preach self-degradation, if they rally the masses against a particular segment of society, if they attempt to limit the individual's freedom or freedom of choice with *any* form of repression, and if they spread fear of God and mistrust toward man, they are not teaching the Truth."

What is Truth?

Andrews: "God is, and man is his Self-expression. When man realizes his identity, a race of gods will rule the universe . . . as Sons and Daughters of the Most High, the Father of All."

CHAPTER FOUR

The Hidden Mystery

It was through Jason Andrews that I first made contact with Elana R., a gentle soul who speaks with the authority of a Master Consciousness.

In our several sessions together we spent much time discussing the loss of spiritual awareness that man once enjoyed. Speaking to me, but referring to all mankind, she said, "Without the awareness of the indwelling One you felt alone and naked in the world. Without the understanding that all things were already yours, ready to be brought forth by your decree, you became trapped in an illusion. You began living in a consciousness of self-preservation with the constant struggle to achieve a previously-known level of livingness that appeared only as a dream in the deep recesses of your mind.

"Throughout recorded history, fully illumined Ones

Bible references from the Gospel According to St. John, Authorized King James Version.

would enter the earth plane in an attempt to break the illusion and reveal the Truth of Man. There would be a brief awakening, but shortly after they returned to the spiritual realm, their teachings would be taken by men still under the hypnotic spell of mortal consciousness and the true meaning was lost once again.

"Here you are today, after countless lives on this planet, seeking the Holy Grail, still searching for the Paradise that was lost. And yet, it has always been with you. You have simply forgotten your identity. You were born initially of Spirit, and you will be born again when you realize Who and What you are. The more you are aware of this indwelling Spirit, the greater the inflow of spiritual energy and power into your mind and heart.

"This Cosmic Consciousness has always been within you, but you have been asleep to it. Now you must awaken. You must feel the warmth of Love in your heart. You must sense the imprisoned Splendor of your True Nature. You must throw open the prison doors and release the Power. Let it be Itself. Let it be *Yourself*! This Life, Light, Power, Love has forever been within you. Even when you fell into the dream of mortality and lost your awareness of the Presence, it did not leave you. No, you left your Self and began a journey into darkness. But even then, the spark of Divine Truth remained in your deeper mind.

"As you turn within and realize the Reality of yourself, that Self fully enters your consciousness and becomes the ruling pattern and principle of your life. But you must realize the Presence. This is the new birth. This is the knowing of Truth on every level of mind, and with every degree of knowingness, more Light is released. The Light is the Christ Presence, the Spirit of Truth. The Divine Spark, hidden in the depths of your soul, becomes the Living Flame of Truth.

"Paul referred to this inner Knowingness as 'the mystery hidden for ages and generations'. He also called it 'Christ in you, the hope of glory'. It is from this illumined Consciousness that you can say . . . 'Father, honor me with the glory that I knew with you before the world was made'."

Why am I here?

Elana: "To be a distributor of God-Power. You must be that through which God may express. Perhaps I should answer your question this way: You are here to rediscover Yourself. You have been living in an imaginary world. Your purpose is to awaken to the Real World. Do this, and the mission of the Master within you can begin. People will then see you in a new light. What happened?— they will ask. They will sense a great change in you because you are becoming You—and a great change will have taken place. But you must take no credit for it. It is the Father within who is doing the work, and if your personal ego expands, it will fill the channel and shut off the flow. Remember that all the entities throughout the universe, including you, were created for just one purpose: to have constant intercommunion with the God-Self, and to be a channel for His manifestation."

You said 'entities throughout the universe'. Are you saying that other planets are inhabited?

Elana: "Could you not believe that in all the worlds in the universe are men, women and children—all in the process of evolving to higher degrees of power? Some are on this planet now assisting in the Awakening, but while they are here, their appearance is not unlike other humans because we see what our consciousness interprets for us . . . as a mental picture of physical form as we know it."

This reminds me of the writings of Konstantin
Tsiolkovsky, who said that there are entities
throughout the universe without physical bodies,
operating from a state of pure consciousness. Are you
talking about these advanced souls?

Elana: "No. Tsiolkovsky was referring to the Universal
Masters, and they do indeed travel from solar system to
solar system. The higher souls in this and other worlds
work with both the seen and unseen Masters. Here, they
are active in selecting suitable channels—to find people
with an open and receptive state of consciousness to
serve the Masters' purposes—so that the message may be
given."

What message?

Elana: "That God is the Self of man, that man is an
expression of his own Selfhood, a spiritual being. The
Reality of you extends from the very Mind of God to the
furthermost point of your awareness and includes all that
you are and have. When you are spiritually illumined,
everything in your life becomes an extension of perfection, even your home, your business, your income, your
relationships. All become spirit in action, spirit in form,
for all is Mind, invisible and visible. The survival of this
planet depends on the recognition of this truth."

**Are you saying that this earth is being colonized by
alien souls who are working with the Masters to save
us from our own self-destruction?**

Elana: "Alien souls? I prefer to think of them as angels
of light—whether from earth or other worlds. They
search, select and guide those men and women who may
be suitable subjects until the time is right, insofar as the
'ripeness' of consciousness is concerned. A Master may
then instruct, or plant the seed of a new concept, which

if allowed to grow, will come forth as a 'new' progressive thought for mankind. And the Word is spread, taking hold and growing in the minds of others, until there is a wave of collective thinking sufficiently powerful to change events and shape the future. Just consider Descartes, Spinoza, Hegel, Emerson, Whitman, Jung, de Chardin, Gandhi, Einstein, William James, Browning, Tennyson, Quimby . . . the names from the past would more than fill a book, and then you would add those who are living today whose thoughts, words and works are penetrating the veil."

Rather than receiving transmissions of thought from the outside, why can't we go within to receive the Word?

Elana: "All true revelations are from within. What you are asking is this: why can we not rely on the inner Christ for all Truth? This, we must do. But, for many there are layers of thought form, hardened negative strata between Self and mind, blocking the Light of Truth. If a person would turn within and seek the Light, the barrier would in time break away. Intuitive powers would develop, strange and wonderful thoughts would enter consciousness, and finally, the Voice of Wisdom within would be heard as the individual 'puts on a new man'. However, the search for the Inner Kingdom may be stimulated from thoughts communicated by the Master Consciousness of another Soul. These divine ideas penetrate into the depths of mind to open a channel for the Light, to open the door to the Spiritual Consciousness. The Truth may then be revealed by the Christ within. All Truth must come from the Spirit of Truth within, but many Souls are active in assisting mankind to find the door to the inner Kingdom. The search for the door to freedom may also begin through an experience of the dark side of the soul, such as a crisis, illness or seeming hopelessness. Regardless of the 'how', man will find the Light. That is his destiny."

Jason says that at least 50-million people on earth now have evolved to the level of the Christ Consciousness. Do you agree?

Elana: "There may be more. The number cannot be fixed, for as the morning light of each new day dispels the darkness of the night, so does the son of man come forth anew to herald a new beginning for a man here, a woman there. The numbers grow daily. The spiritual experience can take place at anytime . . . the veil is parted and the person beholds himself as Christ. As the life of spiritual man is then lived, the individual evolves to masterhood, and still more light is released in the collective consciousness of mankind.

"The illumination . . . the power of the growing light . . . is slowly righting earth, correcting the tilt, bringing it into balance. So few are doing so much, but to the average person, the world appears to be moving toward the final battle. Seen from a fourth dimensional consciousness, however, man is evolving into a new species with undreamed of power . . . and the Illumined Ones have their assignments. Through each risen consciousness, the energy of Mind is moving to establish, reveal universal love, unity and freedom.

"To receptive men and women, new vibrations of health, prosperity, fulfillment, loving relationships, safety and protection, order and harmony begin—perhaps ever so faintly. 'I can be well and strong again' says one. 'I will succeed' says another. A ray of hope at first, then belief, faith in the good. A family relationship is restored, an accident is avoided, a business is stabilized—all seeming miracles under the circumstances. What has happened? The Power of the Living Christ emanating from the Illumined Ones and working through the universal stream of human consciousness has touched the soul of these particular individuals. Such activity is happening daily throughout the world. Once the new vibration of the soul begins, however, it is the responsibility of each person to increase it. We must work out our own salvation. We cannot rely on another person—regardless of his spiritual mastery—to redeem our soul. The continued evolution and advancement must come forth from within."

Would a person in the presence of a highly evolved soul be protected from harm?

Elana: "There is a protective light that may be considered a shield, repelling manifest forces in the immediate situation, even after the sequence of events has gone past the point of no return. If what could have happened through the law of attraction was prevented from happening, the protection would not have been recorded. But if an Illumined Soul comes into the time and space in which the circumstance is already taking place, his consciousness will be a harmonizing influence, and you have heard and read about such situations. Falls from high places with no injury suffered, recovery from 'fatal' bullet wounds, a man walks away from a demolished car on the freeway, a would-be rapist is startled and flees, an assassination attempt fails, a hand literally on fire requires no medication, and the other stories attributed to 'luck'. An Advanced Soul does cast a giant shadow."

Who was the most advanced soul you ever met?

Elana: "Jesus Christ."

The View from the Top.

The greatest Superbeing who ever lived was Jesus Christ. He was the "wayshower"—demonstrating to us what we all can and must become.

Jesus never claimed anything in the name of the personal self, rather He attributed all His works to the Spirit within. As He put it, "He that believeth on me, believeth not on me, but on him that sent me." (John 12:44) This means that you must believe in the same power that worked *through* Jesus—the God-Self within *you.*

Emerson has written, "Jesus Christ belonged to the true race of prophets. He saw with open eye the mystery of the soul. Drawn by its severe harmony, ravished with its beauty, he lived in it, and had his being there. Alone in all history he estimated the greatness of man. One man was true to what is in you and me."

The entire ministry of Jesus was *not* to call attention to himself, but to the Presence and Power within each individual. God, the Power of the Universe, has incarnated Itself in all of us, and Jesus' mission on earth was to reveal this truth. But as Emerson wrote, "what a distortion did his doctrine and memory suffer in the same, in the next, and the following ages!"

Jesus came into the earth plane to teach us about ourselves, and to explain what happened to us. We were like Jesus in our original consciousness. We were constantly aware of our God-Self. This does not mean that we had the *total* God Consciousness of Jesus. He was the complete incarnation of God, and as Charles Fillmore has written, "We cannot separate Jesus Christ from God or tell where man leaves off and God begins in Him." But in our original innocence, we were in a state of higher illumination and superior understanding, and we dwelt in the recognition of the Presence within. Looking within to our True Self, the Reality of us, we could say without hesitation—"I and the Father are one . . . all that the Father is, I am, and all that the Father has is mine."

Since it is a universal Law that consciousness must

55

outpicture itself, we found ourselves with a perfect body and living in a perfect world. Our thoughts were perfect, for they came to us from our Higher Self within, and they were thoughts of peace, joy, abundance, harmony and love. Through the divine inflow, we received the Truth of our being, and our consciousness of Truth became the perfect pattern for the expression of our God-Self. Thus, we truly lived in a Garden of Eden.

But with our free will, we began appropriating ideas of two powers—God and not God, or good and evil. A sense consciousness began forming and later began to rule. Loss of ability to draw constantly on the one and only source of life threw us out of spiritual consciousness—and so, the "fall of man." Since the Law of Mind dictates that our world is a reflection of our consciousness, our lives became a mirror of our negative thoughts. We were forced to work by the sweat of our brow, physical death came upon us, poverty came into existence, and our struggle to rise above the dream-state of error began. In fact, the entire Old Testament tells of man's journey into the wilderness of his soul, and the trials and tribulations in his search for the Light. But the darkness grew stronger and even the spark of remembrance in man's deeper mind was growing cold.

Enter Jesus, the Master Superbeing. His mission was to stir up our memories and remind us who we are and what we can become. He healed the sick, gave vision to the blind, raised the dead, read minds, turned water into wine, multiplied the loaves and fishes, walked on water, calmed the storm, manifested visable money supply—and said that man will do even greater things than he has done. But the great majority of people are still bound by the ills and limitations of the world. Why?

Jesus said that there is light within all men, but men have preferred the darkness to light. He made it very clear—until we turn to the light and are born again, we will not experience heaven on earth.

There is a great deal of talk these days about being "born again." In Jesus' teaching, to be born again is to realize our own identity as a Son of God—just like him! He was (and is) the Self-expression of the Infinite Power of the Universe—just like *you* are. The only difference between you and Jesus is that he fully realized the Truth about himself and you haven't—yet. It is all a matter of degree. He was a Superbeing in perfection. You are one in potential. But never forget one of his most significant statements . . . "I said, ye are gods."

How do we realize our divinity? Jesus said, "You must change your hearts." In modern terms he was saying "Change the patterns in your subconscious mind, because what the subconscious believes is outpictured in your body and affairs." That's why he told us to become like little children. Children are open and receptive . . . a little child knows that he or she is a potential man or woman, and that the role for the next stage of life must be learned. Children are in training for what they will become, but are we? Are we rehearsing our roles as potential Superbeings? Are we learning the techniques, the formulas, the ideas and the discipline to qualify one day to be a Supermind on Planet Earth? Remember, *you* may be the one to tip the scales a little sooner and ring in the New Age of peace on earth and goodwill toward *all* men.

Jesus gave us the clues, the code words and the script to follow, but his teaching has been so clouded in rituals and dogma that the name "Jesus" and the word "church" have been a turn-off for many people.

Understand that Jesus spoke from both His personal and His Christ Consciousness, but when He said "I" and "me"—in almost every instance He was referring to the

Christ living within *your* very own being. Now let's listen to this Master Mind for a few minutes and see what we can learn from His teaching.

"I am Christ, speaking to you now. I am the bread of life; he that cometh to me shall never hunger; and he that believeth on me shall never thirst."

We often "hunger" and "thirst" after more than food and drink, so our inner self is telling us that whatever we need, we must turn within and believe in the Power of our glorious Reality.

"Judge not according to appearances, but judge righteous judgement."

Quit paying so much attention to what is going on around you. It is an illusion, an outpicturing of your beliefs and convictions, so look at things from the vantage point of your Higher Self. See the solution, the answer, the opportunity. Capture the vision of how you would like your life to be—that is judging in the right way.

"I am the light of the world; he that followeth me shall not walk in darkness, but shall have the light of life."

Light means illumination. If you have "seen the light"—you know what to do. There is no more guesswork. You are on a sure path, and the light goes before you so that you will not stumble or fall or make mistakes. If you follow the guidance of your Higher Self, your judgement will be true and you will make the right decisions in every area of your life. Just think of the stress that would be relieved in daily living if you always knew what to do, when to do it, and how.

"If ye continue in my word . . . ye shall know the truth, and the truth shall make you free."

Once you realize (remember) who and what you are, and this truth is embodied within your soul—as a living pattern within your subconscious mind—then you are free. Free to live in accordance with your highest standard . . . free to be, to do, to go . . . free of illness, free of lack and limitation, free of any bondage that could possibly be placed on you in this world.

"I and my Father are one."

Your are one with all the power, wisdom, love, joy, life and substance of the universe. *You* are all that God is in expression!

"I am the way, the truth and the life; no man cometh unto the Father, but by me."

Your spiritual nature, the Superconsciousness within you, is the door to all the good that the Universe has for you. When you realize your true identity, the door swings open and the fullness of power come forth. It goes before you to straighten out every crooked place, it perfects everything that concerns you, and you begin to live the kind of life you were created for.

"And whatsoever ye shall ask in my name, that will I do, that the Father may be glorified in the Son. If ye ask any thing in my name, I will do it."

No qualifications here. When you ask anything in the name of your True Self—*as* your True Self—your request will be granted. If you are thinking that you prayed before and nothing happened, then it was because you were making a demand upon the universe out of a personal consciousness . . . a mental attitude that knows fear and doubt. If you had gotten in tune with the Christ within and had spoken the word from a spiritual consciousness, you would have achieved the results you were seeking. Keep in mind that God holds nothing back from you. He has already given you . . . the Inner You, the fullness of Himself . . . perfect health, lasting prosperity, true-place success, and everything else that is needed in your life to achieve perfect harmony.

". . . the Father . . . shall give you another Comforter, that he may abide with you forever; even the Spirit of Truth."

In several verses, Jesus talks about going away, but that someone else will be given to you, to be with you always. He is saying that once Jesus-the-man completes his mission on earth and returns to the higher spiritual realms, the Christ within *yourself*, living now through your awakened consciousness, will take over.

"the Comforter, which is the Holy Ghost, whom the Father will send in my name, he shall teach you all things, and bring all things to your remembrance, whatsoever I have said unto you."

Now the attention has been transferred to the Living Word within . . . your Teacher, Guide, Helper, Healer, Prosperer, Sustainer, Doer. And now the promise can be fulfilled: "Wherefore if any man is in Christ, he is a new creature; the old things are passed away, behold, they are become new."

"Abide in me, and I in you. As the branch cannot bear fruit of itself, except it abide in the vine; no more can ye, except ye abide in me.

"I am the vine, ye are the branches. He that abideth in me, and I in him, the same bringeth forth much fruit: for without me ye can do nothing.

"If a man abide not in me, he is cast forth as a branch, and is withered; and men gather them, and cast them into the fire, and they are burned.

"If you abide in me, and my words abide in you, ye shall ask what ye will, and it shall be done unto you."

Do you understand? This is your Christ Self talking to you. He is saying that if you will stay in tune with Him and keep the idea of His presence in your mind, then you will be sharing the life of the "vine" and you will bear fruit. The fruits of life are the good things of life . . . everything to make your visit on this planet harmonious and loving and filled with joy. But don't forget the condition: without this Christ Self, you can do nothing. And if you continue "going it alone"—one of these days your life will literally dry up and you will be under the bondage of others. So you have a choice: bondage or freedom. Try to make it without Him and eventually you are going to get burned. Or, team up with that Real You and be free—as you were created to be.

This is not just a figment of someone's imagination. When our minds are directed within to the Christ, the subconscious releases its hold on negative patterns of thought and becomes receptive to the Light, Love and Life of Spirit. When this divine Truth—this Christ Light—becomes the predominant pattern in your subconscious mind, every activity of your life will be an outpicturing of this Ideal, and you will enjoy a continuous and permanent state of joy never before experienced. At least, not since the beginning, when you were fully conscious of yourself as a Son of God in glorious expression.

The Power can work for you only if it can work through you. Repeat that statement to yourself. "*The Power can work for me only if it can work through me.*" And the follow-up thought would be: "*The Power can work through me only when it finds a consciousness that is in tune with its nature.*"

Your good cannot get through your consciousness unless it finds a similar vibration. It cannot move from center to circumference unless it finds something of itself in the human consciousness. God can do *for* you only what He can do *through* you.

So what is the answer? The answer is to unify your human consciousness with your Higher Consciousness to provide an open channel for expression. How do you do this? By becoming aware of the Truth, by understanding the Truth, by knowing the Truth, by feeling the Truth, by speaking the Truth, and by acting in accordance with Truth. And what is the Truth? The Truth is that God *is* your Higher Self—and that He has expressed Himself as your true nature. The "I" of your being is God in expression.

Since the Law states that consciousness *must* outpicture itself, can't you imagine what will happen in your outer world when you fully realize this Truth?

". . . ye shall ask what ye will, and it shall be done unto you."

CHAPTER FIVE

The List

With every degree of understanding, power is released to bring immediate good into your world. And by now, if you have accepted the principles set forth in this book, your awareness and understanding are sufficient to begin making major changes in your life.

The first step is to decide what those changes will be, so put in writing the things, circumstances, situations and experiences that you deeply desire—making certain that there is not anything on your list that would harm anyone else in thought, word or deed.

If you desire a particular healing, increased income or financial independence, fulfillment in your job or a new career opportunity, greater success, more love in your life, companionship, a new home, a new automobile, or whatever—write it down. Then work on your list daily. Revise it, add to it, subtract from it, refine it. If a husband and wife are making lists together, call it the "Family List"—then go and prepare separate lists. And do not put something on your list just because you think you should—put in writing what you *really want.*

Several pages have been provided in this chapter for your lists. Notice the statement at the top of each page:

> *I have the Power within me to realize the fulfillment of each one of these desires. Through the love, wisdom and power of my Supermind, I have the ability to bring about any necessary change in my body or affairs. I believe in my wonderful Inner Self.*

Memorize this statement. Contemplate it as you are preparing your list. Above all, *believe* it.

Don't delay. Begin *now* to put your desires in writing.

I have the Power within me to realize the fulfillment of each one of these desires. Through the love, wisdom and power of my Supermind, I have the ability to bring about any necessary change in my body or affairs. I believe in my wonderful Inner Self.

I have the Power within me to realize the fulfillment of each one of these desires. Through the love, wisdom and power of my Supermind, I have the ability to bring about any necessary change in my body or affairs. I believe in my wonderful Inner Self.

I have the Power within me to realize the fulfillment of each one of these desires. Through the love, wisdom and power of my Supermind, I have the ability to bring about any necessary change in my body or affairs. I believe in my wonderful Inner Self.

CHAPTER SIX

The Secret of Successful Living.

In realizing the fulfillment of desires, the Superbeings have told me—and I have proved it for myself—that you must have the consciousness for the thing desired. Without the consciousness, the thing cannot come to you; with the consciousness, it *must* come.

Emmet Fox, one of the pioneers in the New Thought movement, once said ". . . always the thing you see in the outer is the precipitation on the physical plane of a mental equivalent held by one or more people. The secret of successful living is to build up the mental equivalent that you want; and to get rid of, to expunge, the mental equivalent that you do not want."

What is a mental equivalent? Daniel E., a businessman who has discovered the Power within, calls it a "rock-solid *Conviction*." To Patrick M., a doctor in the higher phases of consciousness development, it is a subconscious *Pattern*. Others call it a Realization, a subjective comprehension of Truth.

And how do you build a mental equivalent for the thing you desire? Since this is truly the key to power and dominion, a great deal of research has gone into the hows and ways of consciousness development. The Superbeings put great emphasis on meditation, affirmations—speaking the word of Truth until it is firmly etched in consciousness, and the technique of creative imagination. All insist that "right thinking" is absolutely necessary, but as Daniel, the businessman, pointed out, "This is not simply a game of positive thinking, nor is it a pollyanna approach to life. It's learning to work with the one Great Power of the Universe, and everyone can be what you call a Superbeing if they adhere to the principles of the teaching and dedicate themselves to achieving mastery over 'this world'."

From conversations with—and communications from —advanced souls, a basic outline was developed for the expansion of consciousness.

1. What do you desire in life? You must focus your thoughts on what you really want.

2. You must make a definite decision to *accept* the fulfillment of your desires.

3. Your desires cannot be fulfilled in the outer world of experience and form unless you have the consciousness or mental equivalent for them.

4. The first step in building the mental equivalent is to recognize that the Divine Idea corresponding to your desire already exists in your Superconsciousness. This is the intellectual awareness.

5. But an intellectual awareness alone does not have sufficient power to shape the outer picture. Your feeling nature must also be brought into play. When the two are combined, a powerful reaction takes place in the subjective phase of mind, setting up a vibration that corresponds to the spiritual equivalent of fulfillment in your Superconsciousness.

6. This fusion of mind and heart along the lines of a particular desire-fulfillment—if protected from thoughts to the contrary—will develop into a conviction. The conviction or mental equivalent becomes the pattern through which the Creative Energy of Mind flows or radiates. As this Energy, Light, Power, Substance passes through the pattern, it takes on all the attributes of the pattern and goes forth into the outer world to manifest corresponding circumstances, experiences and form.

7. Do not outline the way your desire is to be fulfilled—do not be concerned with how your good is to come forth. You must trust the wisdom and ingenuity of the Power, which is God.

8. You develop your subjective convictions through a dedicated program of contemplative meditation, affirmations, and the proper use of your power of imagination.

9. Be filled with a sense of thankfulness and gratitude that your desires are *already* fulfilled (they *are* in Mind), and that they will come forth into visibility at the right time and in the right way.

10. Be active! If you just sit around and wait for your good to fall into your lap, your lap may be far removed from the point of contact and channel that the Power has selected specifically for the outpouring of your good.

Now let's put these ideas into a workable program that will enlarge and uplift your consciousness, so that you may *release* all the good that is already yours.

The Program

In Chapter Five you were asked to make a list of things, circumstances, situations or experiences that you deeply desire. You see, "desire" is the first step in the Action Cycle. It is the bottom rung of the ladder of fulfillment. Without desire, nothing happens. Without desire, the universe and the planet on which we are living would not have been created. Without desire, you would not exist.

Where do desires originate? Desires come forth as an activity of your Higher Self, stirring you up to realize that It wants to do more for you—through you. When you want something that cannot hurt you or anyone else, and will bring good into your life, it is your spiritual Self tugging at your heart's door—trying to get your attention.

Once you have made your list, let's move from desire to decision. For every desire you have, you must make a firm, definite decision to accept the fulfillment of that desire. This is "claiming your good"—or choosing what is to be. Know that the Spirit within you loves a made-up mind, for this is where the pattern of fulfillment begins.

In translating your desires into decisions, you must understand that everything on your list already exists as a Pattern or Ideal in the Mind of your Superconsciousness. To put it another way, *you already have the fulfillment of every desire, otherwise you could not have desired it in the first place.* There is a divine idea corresponding to every form or experience in your life. Right now in the imaging Mind of your Inner Self is the idea of Abundant Prosperity. The Ideal Body is there, too, along with True-Place Success, Right Action, Companionship, Protection, Safety, Beauty, Justice, and whatever else that would correspond to your list of desires . . . automobiles, homes, food, clothing. Remember that nothing in the world could exist unless it was first a spiritual idea. So in truth, you have everything right now. But in order for the Perfect Images to manifest in the material world, you must build a bridge. You must open a channel to release this "imprisoned splendor."

71

You start with recognition.

The Superbeings identify and unify with the Power within and actually become it in expression. They examine every attribute of their Superminds and they see unlimited prosperity, unlimited success, unlimited health, unlimited love, unlimited intelligence, unlimited power, unlimited everything—and they say: "*What you are, I am.*" They saturate their minds and hearts with this truth to such an extent that they constantly think and feel it.

You, too, can begin to build the bridge and open the channel with the very simple act of mentally recognizing that your True Self exists within you now, has everything for you, and will never leave you. Say to yourself:

There is a Presence and a power within me now. It is all knowing, all caring, all loving, all powerful. It is the Completeness of the Universe individualized as me. It is who I am. It is what I am. It is God as me now.

Close your eyes for a moment, relax completely and direct your attention to a point down behind your physical heart and contemplate the idea—"*I am Love.*" Your physical heart really doesn't have anything to do with it, but that region of your body is the seat of your feeling nature, and the warmth, the particular vibration you feel is more of your spiritual nature rising to the surface. You are actually becoming conscious of a Presence within you . . . and the Presence is able to move into your awareness with greater ease through the feeling of Love, which is Its Nature.

You are now one with the Presence and you are beginning to feel the divine energy currents flow in and through you.

Recognize that within that Feeling, which is the Presence, within that Energy Field, is the fulfillment of every desire. Know that right where you are is the Mind of completeness. Let's use "Success[1]" as our Mind Model objective and see how this Truth can be outpictured in our lives. Say to yourself with a feeling of love and joy:

I have made a firm and definite decision in my mind to be wonderfully successful. I now accept the Truth that the spiritual Idea of True Place Success, the Divine Plan for me, is right where I am, in the Mind of my Inner Self. That Self knows Itself to be a unique expression of God. It knows its true worth. That Self is who and what I am. I unify with it. Therefore, I am Success. I am Prosperity. I know that as I recognize and accept the Divine Plan for my life, which is already the Reality of me, it becomes active in my consciousness. I feel its power, its strength, its dynamic urge to manifest itself in my world as new opportunity, as the right job, the ideal career. There is now unity between the inner world of Spirit and the outer world of form. I have embodied the Idea of my True Place in this world. I have claimed my good and it is now interpreting itself as the perfect visible expression of contentment, satisfaction, and joy in the service of others. I am total success. And it is so!

Do you understand what you are doing with this kind of affirmative thought, idea, concept? You are "treating" your subconscious mind—your feeling nature—with a lesson in Truth. And as your subjective nature begins to believe this Truth, it stops believing in boredom, unfulfillment and failure. Your subconscious cannot believe positively and negatively about the same idea at the same time. When it accepts the Truth about you and your True Place Success, it sets up a Success Vibration—a new subjective attitude, a conviction, a mental equivalent that corresponds to the absolute Truth of you.

How do you know when your subconscious accepts a

[1]Use this treatment sequence for other needs such as health, prosperity, companionship—creating your own meditations and affirmations from these examples.

particular Truth idea? When your thinking and feeling nature are in alignment, you are literally filled with Light and *you know that you know.* With a realization there is an inner "click"—and "whereas I was blind, now I can see."

As within, so without.

You must also understand and recognize that there is a universal Law of Cause and Effect operating through you. It is called the Law of Attraction, the Law of Correspondence, and the Law of Consciousness. They are all the same. The Law is actually a Creative Force. It is God substance, the Light of Spirit, a Power that is constantly and forever flowing through you, picking up the particular vibrations of your consciousness and expressing those vibrations in visible form, experience and circumstance. The Power is completely impersonal, and when it flows through your newly developed energy field of success, it has no choice but to manifest your True Place for this point of time in your life. It does not make any difference how badly you have failed in the past, or how many mistakes you have made. It only knows how to create according to your NOW consciousness. But if it flows through a mental atmosphere clouded with ideas of disappointment, resentment and under-achievement, it must, by its very nature, arrange corresponding situations in your life. "As within, so without." "As a man thinketh in his heart, so is he." You are what you think.

Imagination clears the path.

If there were no conflicting subjective thoughts after you completed your "treatment"—the idea would immediately begin to outpicture itself. But if you are like most of us, you have built up quite a reservoir of negative thought patterns. You have kept the door of your mind open to them and have fed them with your thoughts,

The Secret of Successful Living

words and deeds. So these mischievous little thought children have grown strong and have banded together into a gang of mental delinquents. They represent your primary idea of your success in life—or the lack of it—and if you are not "doing what you love and loving what you do"—you know they are doing their job.

Since the Creative Energy flowing from your Higher Self moves through your thought patterns, you must let the divine idea be established as the Master Pattern. This means that you have to protect the "I am Success" idea, keeping it at the center of your being so to speak, while evicting the noisy thieves from your consciousness.

To keep the success idea in position—lined up with the Light—you must call on your power of Imagination. With the proper use of imagination, you "lock in" the idea, much like a slide is secured in a projector. Imagination also "extends" the idea from the center to the circumference of your consciousness, pushing the negative patterns out of the way and providing a clear path for the Power to follow.

In your mind, see yourself truly enjoying your work. See yourself being totally fulfilled in providing a genuine service to others. See yourself joyously moving up the ladder of success professionally, financially, and emotionally. See this picture as a work of art, with you as the artist. Sketch in every detail. Add color to it. Make it a masterpiece! Now feel it in your heart. Love it! Sense the excitement of being the success you want to be right now. Let the waves of enthusiasm roll through you. Feel the utter delight and happiness as you look at your masterpiece. *It's yours!* And it's all here *now.* Don't think about your desires being fulfilled at some later date. They are already fulfilled *right now.* They are fulfilled because you can *see* them fulfilled. And the time-frame between the invisible and visible is only as short or long as the degree of faith and trust in the Power. "He shall give thee the desires of thine heart." "I have ways which will astound you."

After you have devoted a few minutes to your ideal picture, say to yourself:

I now release my masterpiece to my Higher Self, knowing that He will make any necessary adjustments to improve the picture, in order that I may receive all the good that the Universe has for me now. Since I am assured that my desires will be fulfilled according to the Love and Wisdom of my Supermind, my heart overflows with love and gratitude. The feeling of thankfulness pulsates throughout my entire being, and I am filled and thrilled with the joy of life. And it is so!

Go back and read it again—this time *with feeling!*

Keep the Power flowing.

Once you've completed your "treatment"—it's time to move out into the world and do your thing. And as you do, put the idea of success into action. You are going to *live* the idea, and through this living, the Power will be going before you to create new career opportunities for you and new success situations, *but you must get into the main stream of activity*. You cannot sit back and wait for your good to "poof" in front of your eyes, but everything you do, do with ease . . . with poise and confidence and a more relaxed feeling. There is no stress or strain in your new program. A relaxed frame of mind keeps the power flowing smoothly through your Success Vibration, whereas an uptight feeling will restrict the flow. Like putting pressure on a water hose will shut down the flow of water. More pressure, less water. Less pressure, more water. It's all the same principle.

It is suggested that you give yourself three treatments a day—morning, midday and evening. Each treatment should be done with joy and enthusiasm, and last from five to fifteen minutes. Once or twice a week, particularly on Saturday or Sunday, you may wish to spend more time in the visualizing stage to really get the feel of your fulfilled desires. Above all, don't make a treatment a chore . . . don't let it be something you feel pressure to do. To be effective, it must be done in a happy and peaceful frame of mind.

The time between treatments is when most people "fall off the wagon." Let's say you gave yourself a treatment in the early morning hours when the house was quiet. It made you feel powerful, confident and strong— and you began your work-day with a wonderful sense of expectation. But the "rowdy bunch"—those mental delinquents we talked about earlier—decide to cause a little trouble in your consciousness. First you feel an uneasy feeling in the pit of your stomach, followed by such a thought as "I'll never get ahead in this job"—or—"I'm afraid that . . ."—or—"I'll never be able to do it"—or some other negative intruder.

Remember that when you finished your treatment, the creative energy was flowing through your divine idea and was moving into the outer world to accomplish its mission. But when the mischievous ones come back into your mental household, they begin to block the light and try to dislodge the divine idea from its firm position in your mind. If they succeed, the Power is actually diverted from the fulfillment pattern and channeled through the negative thought form. The result: Your good is cancelled out and the false beliefs are again externalized.

So your objective between treatments is to protect your ideal mind model with tender loving care and to keep your Light shining. You do this with continued use of affirmations. A strong affirmation, repeated silently or audibly when fear or doubt arises, begins to build a protective cover around your divine idea, while maintaining the energy flow in the right direction. Affirmations also scatter the "wild bunch" and if continued persistently— will keep away all negative thoughts and emotions contrary to your divine idea.

Here are three affirmations that we have found effective in dealing with negative thoughts and fear:

My True Self wants me to have the fulfillment of my desires, and nothing can stand in the way of His Infinite Power.

The Law of the Spirit is manifesting my divine idea here and now, and my good is flowing to me in streams of plenty.

I have incredible confidence in myself to keep the channel open for the manifestation of my desires.

It is best to create your own affirmations, based on a deep feeling of Truth. And in some cases, the shorter the affirmation the better. To find the right affirmation for the moment, simply say the opposite of what you are thinking and feeling—until you feel a sense of peace. Then you know the mischievous ones have gone on their way.

Of course, if these mental delinquents have completely taken over your consciousness, then you will have to do some major house-cleaning. And usually the first step in the cleansing process is to get rid of all unforgiveness. This does not mean running around telling everyone you are sorry when you are not. The word "forgive" means simply to "give up"—so you start cleaning up your mind by giving up all grudges and negative feelings toward others. All others. *Everyone!* Without exception. If you are holding any negative feelings about any individual or any group of people, stop right where you are, stir up that feeling of love within you and say "*I*

*forgive you totally and completely. I hold no unforgiveness in
my heart toward anyone, and if there is anything in my subconscious mind that resembles unforgiveness, I cast it upon
the indwelling Christ to be dissolved right now. I forgive everyone and I am free."*

As we probe deeper into our consciousness, we may
see other negative thoughts hanging on for dear life.
There's old Mr. Fear lurking in the background. You certainly don't want him around because you can't fear anything and also enjoy the experience of joyful living. So
call in the Power of the Presence and evict him now.

Ah, but there's a greenish hue of jealousy still remaining, plus a few mental delinquents called resentment,
condemnation, prejudice, selfishness, guile, futility, de-
ceit, inadequacy, impatience, irritation, and rejection.
Getting rid of all of these delinquents one by one could
be quite a chore, so let's just sweep them out all at once.
"I call on the Law of Spirit now to arrest these intruders
and take them out of my consciousness, out of my life,
permanently. I don't need them. I don't want them. I
will not have them!"

Now sit back and wait a few minutes for the Law to do
its cleansing work.

If one particular member of the rowdy bunch returns
to pester you, develop your own affirmation of Truth and
speak the word with great feeling—then watch as a
powerful ray of spiritual energy totally eliminates the
bandit from your consciousness.

Only *you* can work on your consciousness, because
only *you* know where the soft spots are. There are people
in Truth today who are praying, treating and meditating
without achieving results. And the reason is that they
have failed to take the cleansing action. They want all
the good that is rightfully theirs without clearing the
channel for its outpouring—but the Law just doesn't
work that way.

Not of This World.

You must never forget that whatever you hold in consciousness as the truth about yourself and God will be mirrored in the world about you. If you think there is good and evil, there will be. If you think that God can withhold your good from you, it will be held back. If you think you can be sick, you will be. If you think you will fail, you will surely do so. If you think of yourself as just a "human being" subject to the winds of fate, you will ride that rollercoaster all of your life, high one day and low the next, healthy and sick, plenty of money during "good" times and desperately in need of cash when times are "bad", harmony followed by disorder, happiness and dispair, peace and turmoil.

"But I'm only human," you may say. "Everybody gets sick, or has an accident once in a while, or runs low on money, or has a blow-up with a neighbor."

The idea that you are "only human" is simply not true—and neither are you supposed to lead a less-than-perfect life on earth. Jesus said that we all are gods, and that it was the Father's good pleasure to give us the Kingdom. This means that we are Sons of an Infinite King, living in a Kingdom of Heaven right now on earth. Just because we don't know this doesn't change the fact.

"But what about my back and the payment on the car that's past due and the unfair way I'm being treated at the office. Don't tell me I'm in heaven. It's more like hell."

Then it is a hell that you and you alone have created. If you are flopping around in the water about to drown, don't blame the water—blame the problem on the fact that you do not know how to swim. If you are having any kind of problem, do not condemn the situation or circumstance. Face yourself squarely in the mirror and acknowledge that you have been plugged into the race mind, which is nothing but the carnal consciousness of mankind, and declare that you have had enough of this mass illusion. Stake your claim to your inheritance, which is the Kingdom, and to the Truth of your being, which is the Spirit of God. Now dedicate yourself to pulling the plug on mortal limitations and rising into a new consciousness of Power and Dominion.

This is what the saints, the mystics, the masters and the Superbeings have done. And this is what men and women just like you are doing. Behind closed doors in offices throughout this country, managers and executives are contemplating Truth ideas. In countless homes, husbands, wives and young people are affirming and visualizing their good. Glance at a bookshelf in an office or home and chances are you'll see—in addition to the Bible—books by such authors as Ernest Holmes, Charles Fillmore, Joel Goldsmith, J. Sig Paulson, Emmet Fox, Tom Johnson, Catherine Ponder, Robert A. Russell, Ralph Waldo Trine, Ernest Wilson, Marcus Bach, Ervin Seale, James Dillet Freeman, Jack H. Holland, Joseph Murphy, Eric Butterworth, Emilie Cady, and many other spiritual leaders who are doing their part to lead us all back to the High Road of Truth.

The individuals who are realizing the Presence and Power of God within are saying, "I live in this world, but I am not of it. I do not accept anything but peace, power and perfection—and this consciousness of the Ideal is outpictured in my world."

You can say the same thing. Identify yourself with Yourself and step out in mastery. Dare to rise above the sickness, lack, depression, discord and unfulfillment of mortal man and become the Person you were created to be. Do it now. Every day you wait is a day delayed—and every day delayed puts you that much further behind in realizing the wonder and joy of life.

As Thoreau put it, "If one advances confidently in the direction of his dreams, and endeavors to live the life

which he has imagined, he will meet with a success un-
expected in common hours. He will put something behind, will pass an invisible boundary; new, universal,
and more liberal laws will begin to establish themselves
around and within him, or the old laws will be expanded
and interpreted in his favor in a more liberal sense; and
he will live with the license of higher order of beings."

The license of a higher order of beings. Isn't that what we
all want?

CHAPTER SEVEN

The Way of Health

Patrick M., an M.D. specializing in family practice, says that a growing number of doctors agree that there is a healing power within man, and that it is possible for this power to maintain the body in perfect condition. He said, "I, personally, believe that this spiritual life-stream will keep the body in a state of perfection when man realizes the unreality of disease."

The unreality of disease. A strong statement for a medical doctor who daily sees an endless parade of patients with some form of illness or suffering. But Patrick M. is no ordinary doctor. He is a Superbeing who also happens to have found his true place in the medical profession. Doctor M. believes that all body malfunctions are the result of negative patterns lodged in the subconscious mind. Don't talk to him about viruses or bacteria or heredity. Do so and he will counter with a discussion of fear patterns, emotional instability and mental conflicts.

"I treat the cause as much as I do the effect," he said.

"Without over-simplifying it, you could say that high blood pressure, for example, may be an indication of a subjective pattern laced with feelings of irritation, resentment and criticism. The common denominators of most illnesses, in my opinion, are confusion, fear, resentment, futility, hostility and irritation. As we replace these 'bugs' with healing thoughts, they are cast out and the body resumes its natural harmonious functioning. Nature's built-in life support system, if not tampered with, will maintain the body in an ideal state."

Dr. M. is not alone in his thinking. Behavioral medicine has become a major field of study by an increasing number of physicians throughout the country. Medical researchers at such institutions as John Hopkins University School of Medicine, the University of Southern California, and Yale University are agreeing that *emotions* are the primary factor in illness. And in tracking a disease from its manifest state back through the body to the mental distress that set off the physical imbalance, they are finding deepseated patterns of anxiety, grief, anger, depression and fear. In thousands of case histories the evidence is clear: the body does reflect the state of an individual's emotions.

Holistic Healing

There is a definite trend in the medical profession to shift the focus from the repair of the physical mechanism to an improvement of the functioning of the whole human being. This is the "holistic" approach to medicine, where the doctor considers the total interrelationship of mind, body and spirit in creating a state of well-being in the individual. Part of the inspiration for this movement is the growing understanding that there is a healing principle within man that is the cause of his physical expression.

But we need to go further than this and realize that

the Creative Mind that is individualized *as* man has no conception whatsoever of disease. This Mind is the Will of God in individual expression, and it sees and knows only perfection. Within its consciousness is the idea of the perfect body, and this Ideal Pattern is constantly seeking to renew the body after Itself. Science knows that every cell in the body is periodically renewed, so it is only logical to state that it is *consciousness* that alters the cells according to our thoughts and emotions.

"The body reflects the mind," says Dr. M. "When the mind is in tune with its Christ nature it becomes harmonious, and this state of consciousness will maintain order in the bodily functions. Disorder in the mind will disturb the equilibrium of the body."

So again, mind is the answer! If you can see your body as your True Self sees it, your body will respond accordingly. If you can understand that your life is God's Life, and that God's Life is perfect, then you can realize that the life form you are cannot embrace sickness or decay.

Preventive Medicine

To enjoy perfect health, you must choose and accept it. You must tune in to the Superconsciousness within you and let its healing power be released into every cell and organ of your body. Be conscious of the Life Force flowing through you. Feel its soothing, healing currents of divine love and know that every function of your physical being is whole and complete. Embody the idea of perfect health in your consciousness and you will be restored, renewed and revitalized after the Perfect Pattern within.

Dr. M. makes an interesting observation: "I have seen miraculous healings . . . terminal cancer disappearing without a trace and other instantaneous 'cures' by what must be considered spiritual means. Many of these people were able to turn within, tune in, and release the healing power by effecting a change in consciousness. What puzzles me is this. If they were already advanced in consciousness to the point where the Divine Law of Adjustment could be called into play on such short notice, why did they let themselves become vulnerable to the disease in the first place? We should not wait until the body breaks down to practice spiritual health. We must let the Christ live through us each day of our lives. This is true preventive medicine."

How do we do this? Follow the treatment sequence discussed in Chapter Six, substituting "health" for "success." Accept the Truth that you are perfect and build the mental equivalent that nothing can touch your body except the direct action of God, and God is Love. Understand that God does not *give* you health . . . God *is* your health. Since you are one with Wholeness and Perfection, that must be the true state of your being.

Lift up your vision. See yourself as God sees you— radiantly healthy and filled with joy and peace. See yourself doing everything you want to do . . . energetically, enthusiastically and easily. See yourself smiling, laughing and expressing a new zest for living. Visualize your body as a dynamic vehicle for every physical expression that you enjoy doing, and see yourself demonstrating a wonderful sense of well-being. And most of all, keep your mind free of all thoughts of confusion, fear, resentment, futility, hostility and irritation. Fill your consciousness with love, joy, peace, and gratitude.

Remember that twenty-four of Jesus' thirty-three miracles were related to the healing of the body. Also recall that He said, "He who belives in me will also do the works that I do; and greater works than these will he do." He is telling you that you can realize the healing principle if you put your trust in your indwelling Christ. He is saying that you, too, can heal if you believe in the Power of the Christ Mind within you. You can heal yourself—

you can heal others—you can be a healing influence to all those within the range of your consciousness.

But remember the condition . . . "He who believes in me . . ." You must *believe* WHOLE-heartedly if you are to reveal the healing Truth. To do this you must replace error concepts of disease and convictions of imperfection with ideas based on the Reality of you . . . whole, perfect, complete. To be healed and to enjoy radiant health on a continuous basis, you must introduce new affirmative thoughts into your consciousness . . . you must "change your mind" about your body.

Meditate daily on this Perfect You, and speak your word of healing with authority as Jesus did—regardless of what the condition appears to be.

Live the Truth of Health

After your meditation, go about your business with an uplifted consciousness of health and well-being. And remember, you have to *live* the truth of health. You cannot reprogram your consciousness on the mental level and expect it to remain open as a channel for the healing power if you do not continue your health work in the manifest world. This means that you cannot maintain a consciousness of health unless there is continuity between what you think and how you act. If you affirm a perfect body and then fail to exercise and diet properly, or eat the right foods, you are not practicing health.

Understand that exercise and diet will not necessarily promote good health. Rather, they may help you in the development of a *health consciousness*. And that's the key! You take whatever action in the outer world that will give you a greater sense of well-being, greater confidence in the natural functioning of your body, a more positive attitude toward the physical you. Remember that your body is an outpicturing of your deeper mind. It is a mirror image of what you sincerely believe about yourself, and your subconscious mind is constantly monitoring your beliefs. So if you affirm one thing and act in a different manner, the actions will speak louder than words and you will cancel out your good. In effect, you will be telling your subconscious to disregard the previous instructions and to continue believing in a less-than-perfect body.

For example, you affirm and visualize a body filled with great energy and vitality, but then you position yourself primarily on your posterior most of the day at home or in the office, overindulge in food and drink, get too little (or too much) sleep, and then complain because you are tired and not feeling very well. You've simply got to tie it all together—thought and action—if you want the creative concept of health to work.

The same holds true in reverse. You can jog five miles a day, eat only natural foods, take the limit of vitamins and minerals—and spend your days agitated, resentful, fearful and wondering why you are not enjoying good health. Science has now traced eighty percent of all ailments to the way we think, and it will not be long before that figure is 100 percent. Five miles of jogging may not cancel out five minutes of hostility. And all the vitamins on the shelf simply will not overcome the physical damage caused by daily doses of resentment and unforgiveness.

You have got to get your *whole* act together in order to enjoy the radiant health that is your divine birthright. And never for a minute doubt that you can be healed of any disease. The Power within can cure a cancer as easily as a cold, but in order to readjust your bodily functions, it must flow through your consciousness. If the Power flows through a mental household littered with fear of living, or a fascination with illness, or a condemning heart—then it must duplicate or maintain that state of mind in your body. Your body reflects your mind. It is the physical image of your mental atmosphere. Now you can understand why some mental house-cleaning will be necessary if your body is not everything you want it to be.

Should you visit a doctor if you are ill? Of course, if that is where you are in consciousness. And if you are not *sure* of your realization of the healing principle, combine medical assistance with spiritual healing treatments. Above all, do not try to demonstrate beyond the level of your consciousness. God may have to work through the physician and through you while you are working to correct the alignment of your soul. But once you have completed your mental cleansing and have realized the truth of health, you may never see a doctor again except on the golf course.

HOW THE BODY REFLECTS THE MIND

SUBCONSCIOUS PATTERNS OF	MAY MANIFEST AS
ANGER—HOSTILITY	Appendicitus, arthritis, boils, constipation, heart problems, high blood pressure, indigestion, inflammation
CONFUSION—FRUSTRATION	Colds, flu, headache
CRITICISM	Arthritis, liver problems, ulcers, high blood pressure
FEAR	Accidents, asthma, flu, headache, heart problems, indigestion
GRIEF—DEPRESSION	Cancer, colds, gallstones
GUILT—SELF-CONDEMNATION	Back trouble, cancer, hay fever
LACK—LIMITATION	Anemia, asthma, kidney trouble
OLD AGE CONCERN (afraid of growing old)	Hardening of arteries, kidney trouble
RESENTMENT—UNFORGIVENESS	Arthritis, cancer, heart problems
TENSION—STRESS	Colds, constipation, headache, high blood pressure

A word about age

The true Superbeings throughout the world are literally reversing the aging process. They have realized that the indwelling Reality cannot grow old, cannot age, cannot die—that the True Self of each individual lives in a perpetual state of eternal youthfulness. Since this is true, there must be an idea corresponding to this divine nature in the mind of each Superconsciousness. The advanced souls have recognized this idea and have appropriated it into their consciousness. The Law then works through this divine Pattern to slow down, stop, and reverse the aging process and reflect a younger and more vibrant appearance.

Never forget that *what the mind can conceive and believe, the mind can achieve.*

Write your own health affirmations as daily reminders.
For starters . . .

1. My life is God's Life and God cannot be sick.

2. Through the healing currents of Love flowing from the Christ within, I am now whole and complete.

3. I believe that my body is the outpicturing of a divine idea, the expression of a Perfect Pattern within, and therefore I am whole and in perfect health.

4.

CHAPTER EIGHT

The Way of Wealth

An Associated Press story appearing in newspapers in early 1981 was headlined: "Money worries those at the top, new survey says." The article pointed out that "executives are not only genuinely concerned about inflation and the erosion of their wealth, but also are uncertain what steps to take to preserve it." The survey was based on interviews with 200 executives with incomes ranging from $40,000 to $200,000 a year in six cities. Fifty-five percent of the executives said they did not expect a higher standard of living in the future.

Now if people in the $40,000–$200,000 category are worried about their finances, what about the great majority of families who are struggling to get along on much less? Could it be that their quiet desperation and inner turmoil is being outpictured by a shattered family life, a greater number of divorces, an alarming trend in white collar crime, and needless disease in mind and body?

The gut-wrenching feeling of lack and limitation can

blow peace of mind and harmony right out the window, and can bring on more discord and discontent than almost any other race mind condition. It has destroyed families, cities and nations, and until man realizes that abundance is his divine inheritance, he will continue to live in the sin of poverty or as the prodigal son eating the husks in a far country.

Of course, money itself will not necessarily make a person happy—but a prosperity consciousness will bring forth poise, confidence, contentment, peace, joy, and freedom from the fear of lack—in addition to tangible supply. So money without the consciousness for it is not our objective. What we want is a spiritual understanding that God is our all-sufficiency of supply in all things. Thus, money becomes a spiritual experience when we work with the principle.

It is interesting that people who have evolved in consciousness to where they can truly be called Superbeings have little concern for demonstrating supply. And the reason is because they recognize that they are the boundless wealth of the Universe in expression . . . they know they are related to the One Mind and that this Mind is their inexhaustible Resource. The result: They attract all good things to them in overflowing measure and continually experience the joy of abundant living. They let their minds speak for them, and each consciousness makes its own particular demand on the universal treasury.

How rich can you be? As rich as you think you can be, or as wealthy as your contentment level. However, most people are content in just "getting by"—and if that is as far as your consciousness can expand, then so be it. *You* have made that choice. But know that you can achieve the total freedom of financial independence if you choose it and will work to uplift your consciousness to accomodate that level of completeness. When Jesus told us to seek the Kingdom, He didn't say to try for a little bit of the Kingdom or half of the Kingdom. He said to go for it in its entirety . . . to incorporate the total spiritual consciousness of plenty in our hearts. And He said to do this *first*—and then all things would be added (attracted) to us.

When we realize the presence of God within us, that realization is a spiritual experience . . . it is the Kingdom of Heaven (Harmony) within you. And out of this Kingdom—this spiritual consciousness—flows everything that we could desire in this life.

Abundance is Your True Nature.

Daniel E. is an individual who has found the Kingdom. Having experienced poverty as a child and seeing first-hand its destructiveness, he decided at an early age to dedicate his life to achieving great wealth.

Several failures later he gave up in despair, and at one point even considered taking his own life. But out of the sorrow of this depression, out of the darkness of total futility, a voice within him said, "I am the good which you seek." From that moment on, Daniel followed the echo of the voice into the depths of his consciousness until he found the Door to the inner Kingdom. As it opened, the voice said, "Behold, I make all things new." *This was the Experience. This was the Realization.* And all things in Daniel's life were indeed made new.

An idea to benefit others was quickly turned into a successful new business venture and a whole new life of high prosperity began. His creative ideas continue to yield fantastic dividends and money is attracted to him in abundant measure. Daniel calls his concept of prosperity the "Will of Wealth"—but I didn't realize the purely spiritual basis for his philosophy until we met. I just assumed he had one of those superhuman talents for acquiring wealth, and one of my first questions was . . .

Do you have a particular formula or technique for creating prosperous conditions in your life?

Daniel: "I do not create anything. All the wealth that mankind could use for eternity has already been created. God has provided us with such lavish abundance that if the whole kingdom exploded into visibility now, there would not be room to store it all on earth. I am referring to God substance, the Power, the pure energy of Divine Mind that is formed by the consciousness of man."

This substance or creative energy flows through the mind of man and reproduces his beliefs as form and experience. Correct?

Daniel: "Yes. Substance—the thought energy of God —is the reality of everything visible. It is the wealth, the treasury of the spiritual realm. We live, move and have our being in it. Substance pours itself through us at every moment and externalizes itself as a mirror of our convictions. When you have a feeling of financial well-being, you are feeling the energy of substance."

How have you developed and maintained your particular prosperity consciousness?

Daniel: "In order for something to be active in your life, you must be aware of it. To be aware of something is to have an idea of it. When I think of substance as all-providing abundance, this thought is the idea, and when I feel the reality of the idea, I am developing a consciousness of substance. This is the only true prosperity consciousness."

Then the first step is to implant the idea of substance in our consciousness.

Daniel: "You already have it. Substance is the divine idea underlying all visible manifestation—and that idea is focused, impressed on your soul at this very moment.

It is there with all of the other divine ideas that make up your spiritual consciousness. But until you provide an outlet for that idea, in other words, recognizing that the idea already exists as a part of your true nature and embodying it within your feeling nature, spirit will flow through some other concept, one that believes only in materiality. Subjective thinking on the material level judges by appearances and fails to understand that all wealth, all prosperity is spiritual, directly related to God Mind. When pure spiritual energy flows through an idea that is based on a materialistic universe, the energy conforms to that concept and is subject to the race mind beliefs in lack, limitation, shortages, and having to 'earn a living'.

"However, as the substance idea is understood and realized, every need of supply in the physical world is made manifest. Substance—flowing through a consciousness of substance—'reads your needs' as it passes through your mind and literally becomes the needed thing, whether money, a home, an automobile, or whatever.

"Look at it this way. God, the infinite Consciousness of the universe, expresses Itself as you, as me, as everyone. If Consciousness expresses Itself, what is Its expression? Consciousness, of course. Consciousness expresses Itself as consciousness, Mind expresses Itself as mind, Spirit as spirit, Life as life, God as God. So the expression of God *as* you is your spiritual *consciousness*, your true nature. This spiritual consciousness is the inlet for the full focus of God Mind. Your true nature has within it the Wisdom of the ages and all of the other attributes of the Parent Mind including divine substance. Being conscious of itself, it is conscious of substance as the spiritual essence, the creative energy, behind all visible manifestation. Therefore, it knows itself to be the infinite Abundance of the universe—individualized! And what it knows, it becomes—if nothing is put in its way.

This is why you must bridge the gap between outer manifestation and the inner Storehouse with ideas of Truth.
If you know that according to principle, consciousness
must outpicture itself, and if you know that your true
self, the I AM of you, is a consciousness of lavish abundance—then you know you must let that consciousness
become a part of your feeling nature. It is bringing the
true I AM of you out of the depths of deep inner space
and into your heart. It is taking the indwelling Christ as
your all-sufficiency and letting it take its rightful place in
your consciousness."

**What you are really saying is that we must look only
to God for our money, our homes, or whatever else we
need.**

Daniel: "God does not give us money or homes. He
gives us Himself. He gives us substance, and substance
becomes the money or the home. If we look to God for
material things without understanding that substance is
the underlying cause, we are leaving out the secret ingre-
dient in prosperity demonstrations. We are working
strictly for the effect and overlooking the cause. Through
pure mental work you may be able to bring forth money,
but you will not be able to maintain prosperity without
the spiritual foundation."

**How do we tune into the Prosperity Consciousness
that is already a part of our nature?**

Daniel: "By daily meditating on the truth that this
consciousness of abundance is already within you, and by
contemplating the creative substance that is continually
flowing from this creative mind. Know that substance is
wealth, substance is prosperity, substance is abundance.
Recognize that the idea of overflowing supply, lavish
abundance, is a part of your true nature. Remember that
you are God in expression . . . God expressing Himself.

As God brings the whole thrust of Himself into individual expression, He does not leave a part of Himself behind. The fullness of the Presence individualizes as you, and that includes the Infinite Bank of the Universal Treasury.

"Your spiritual consciousness understands substance as all-sufficiency . . . an abundance for every need. You, too, must look to God substance as the fulfillment of your needs. Accept the idea that abundance is yours. Bring the idea into your consciousness. Contemplate it. Love it. Bless it. Be grateful for it. It is the 'X Factor'. It is the missing link. It is the foundation stone of prosperity that was prepared for you in the beginning."

What happens when a person works with the substance idea—in other words, working spiritually for prosperity—while still maintaining a degree of materiality in consciousness?

Daniel: "Recall that I said that substance 'reads your needs' as it passes through your consciousness. If you think of your needs as already fulfilled—and you would with a spiritual consciousness—substance will manifest fulfillment. But with a degree of materiality, as you put it, you may feel that there is a possibility that your needs may not be fulfilled. Depending on the intensity of your feeling, substance will either mirror and magnify slow progress, or a definite lack in your world. You hope for the best, but you're just not sure you are going to get it. A material consciousness is always uncertain, while a spiritual mind always operates on the basis of absolute certainty.

"Let's suppose that you desire a new home. Your Higher Self understands that man in his present state of development has many needs and desires in the physical world—including that of shelter—so 'before they call, I will answer'. In other words, Creative Mind has already

99

given you the raw material (substance) and the power to shape it according to your highest vision.

"The idea of a new home, surrounded and protected with the strength of faith, will come forth into visibility. Why? How? Because you are combining the cause factor with the effect you desire. You are blending the idea of substance and its unfailing principle of productivity with the idea of a new home. Do you see that if you have an idea for something you wish to possess or experience, in essence you already have the fulfillment of the desire? In this case, the substance *is* the home, and the home is the substance in form.

"You place the image of the home in the stream of substance and the substance flows from the invisible to the visible—according to the degree of your faith and expectation. Substance has a plastic quality, and what you impress it with, it becomes. So expect the very best home you can imagine."

What is the best way to impress substance?

Daniel: "You impress substance by choosing clearly what you want, affirming that your desire is already fulfilled in spirit, visualizing the fulfillment, releasing the substance to do its perfect work, and acting on any ideas that come to you. With these steps followed faithfully and gratefully, substance *must* manifest accordingly. The mental pictures of your heart's desires will be objectified."

When you say "objectified"—you cannot mean that our desires will suddenly materialize in front of us. Please explain how they are fulfilled.

Daniel: "Do not be too concerned with the *how*. While it is true that a new home—to use the previous example—will not suddenly appear in the back yard of your present dwelling, events and circumstances will take place enabling you to acquire the home you desire. If you do not have the down payment, a way will be worked out for you to have it. If you want more home than you can afford at the present time, a way will be shown to enable you to quickly bring your income up to the required level. And a home that fits all of your requirements down to the last detail will be brought to your attention. Once you let the abundance idea—your true nature—enter your subconscious mind . . . once your feeling nature beings to pulsate with the Truth that you are heir to the wealth of the universe . . . be prepared for an incredible turn of events. God works in mysterious ways to perform His wonders, so let the 'way' of externalized abundance be totally in His hand.

"I have seen too many demonstrations of this Truth to ever doubt it. I've watched the owner of a small business on the brink of bankruptcy suddenly turn everything around and attract more customers than he could handle at the time. How? By practicing the Presence of God as his unfailing supply and daily affirming prosperous conditions. A friend of mine credits the building of a major multi-million dollar company to the daily practice of creative imagination. In my particular case, I took the Inner Man, The God Self I am in truth, as my partner— and we work *together* to accomplish his Grand Plans."

Why do you call your particular philosophy the "Will of Wealth?"

Daniel: "Because it is the Will of God for man to be rich and enjoy the abundant life."

If we compare Daniel's methods with the other Superbeings as discussed in Chapter Six, we see a similar working pattern. The consensus is to:

1. Identify with your God-Self (meditate daily on substance).

2. Claim and accept your good (choose what you want).

3. Build the mental equivalent (affirm your good).

4. Lift up your vision (visualize the fulfillment).

5. Release the picture (let the substance do its work).

6. Be thankful (follow the steps gratefully).

7. Live your demonstration (act on any ideas that come to you).

Based on our research, it seems that the *acting* part may be the most difficult, so let's spend a few minutes on this phase of the program.

First of all, you must capture the feeling you would have if your desires were fulfilled right now—and go about your day with that joyful, thankful attitude. Don't judge by appearances. Fret not over how things seem. Let your actions be based on the Truth that you are the image and likeness of God and therefore, there is no good thing missing in your life. You are complete! So act the part. Acting is not pretending. "Act" means to *do, function, execute, operate, move, press on, put forth, commit yourself.* Let your actions be based on the knowledge of Who and What you really are!

Regardless of the kind of job you have, begin now to do more than has been expected of you. Make a list of everything that needs to be done and tackle each project with enthusiasm, knowing that the more you do today, the more time you will have for "something new and exciting" that is coming your way tomorrow. Then do the same thing tomorrow.

Be open and receptive to the Voice within speaking to you through your intuition. If you feel an urge to call someone, write a letter, or make a visit—do so. You never know just how, when or where your Inner Self is going to manifest as your abundance, so these hunches may be the first link in a chain reaction that will pay off in handsome dividends.

A new money-making idea may also pop into your mind, and it is important that you immediately write down every detail. As you do, you'll find the "way and the means" to develop and execute the idea flowing through your mind as you write. Then move into action with the idea, but don't consider this flash of inspiration as the only channel for your good. Stay open! You will be amazed at the offers of assistance from strangers, the ideas given to you by friends and co-workers, the check in the mail you didn't expect, a new opportunity with a compensation package that you would have considered unbelievable before you started your prosperity program. It is all part and parcel of the activities of the great Law of Abundance.

After talking to Daniel, I sought the advice of several other Superbeings regarding prosperity demonstrations, and here are a few of their secrets:

1. Do not tell anyone that you are working on prosperity from a spiritual-mental approach. If you do, you will break the connection and drain the power building up in and around your new mental equivalent. Secrecy is an absolute essential.

2. Understand that you are not trying to make anything happen. You are simply *releasing* the abundance that is already a part of your True Nature. Eliminate all pressure and intensity. *Let* the substance flow into visibility and experience. Easy does it!

3. As your good begins to materialize, do not get "puffed up" with spiritual pride. Remember, *you* are not doing the work. It is spiritual substance that is interpreting itself as the fulfillment of your desires, and you are but the channel for its outpouring.

4. Critical thoughts and feelings of fear will hold back your good, while a consciousness of love and trust will speed up the flow. Love is the fulfillment of the Law, and Faith is the energy that clears the channel.

5. Acknowledge the Spirit within as the *one Source* of abundance—the one Source of your supply. Look *only* to God for your prosperity.

6. Do not outline the way your good is to come forth. Let the Spirit surprise you with Its delightful ways of showering you with abundance.

7. Recognize that it is the Will of God for you to be wealthy. Understand that there is not anything that even resembles lack, limitation or poverty in His Consciousness. You were born to be rich! You are the offspring of the Infinite Abundance of the Universe.

8. Do not delay your demonstration by holding in mind the idea of receiving your good "tomorrow." God works in the *now*. "*Now* is the accepted time." If you live in the future, your prosperity will always be one day ahead of you.

9. Abundance in the physical world is an outpicturing of a prosperity consciousness, so work from within. The higher your consciousness, the greater your prosperity. As above, so below.

10. Gratitude and thanksgiving are vital ingredients in developing a prosperity consciousness. Nothing opens the door to the Storehouse as quickly as a thankful heart.

11. You develop a prosperity consciousness by changing your mind—by replacing ideas of lack with ideas of abundance. Spend more time each day thinking about what you want rather than what you do not want. You don't want lack so stop thinking about it.

12. Keep your money circulating. If you horde it for a rainy day, you may have to spend it all on an ark.

Remember that you are not embarking on a spiritual program of abundance just to "get" money, homes or cars. You are seeking, through a prosperity consciousness, the freedom to be Yourself without any concern or anxiety over financial matters. You want to be free to do, to go, to be according to your highest vision. And when you help yourself, you become a prospering influence for everyone.

Recall the words of Jason Andrews . . . "The good of the whole must begin with the good of the individual . . . you help the world when you help yourself . . . we are all one, all waves in the same ocean, and one man's consciousness of abundance and well-being with its outer manifestations releases more light into the race consciousness for the benefit of all. So start with yourself."

Why not begin right now?

Write your own prosperity affirmations as daily reminders.

For example . . .

1. I am not content with just "getting by". I choose the total freedom of lavish abundance.

2. I recognize divine substance as the source of my abundance and it is manifesting for me now.

3. I am rich and free, as I was created to be.

4.

CHAPTER NINE

The Ultimate Way

We are seeking wholeness and completeness, but our faith and expectations may be more active in one particular area than another. One person may conceive of a well body, realize the truth of health, and have that pattern working on the subjective level. But the prosperity idea may be slower in coming because of deep negative conditioning in this or another life. Or another may be wonderfully wealthy, with great love and companionship, only to be bothered and burdened with a body that is not functioning according to the divine design.

Some of the Masters say that we should work on one ideal at a time, breaking up the old negative patterns and replacing them with a new mind model so that we may demonstrate outwardly the Truth of Being in that particular area of our lives—then move on to the next priority. Others insist that this is the roundabout way to the mountain top, and that by practicing the Presence, we will realize our true identity much sooner, thus embody-

107

ing the Christ Mind and the completeness of life that this Consciousness represents.

The right method depends on where you are in consciousness and what you're willing to settle for. As one Advanced Soul pointed out, ". . . some of us are faced with a crucial choice which dominates this entire incarnation: what are we willing to settle for? Are we willing to settle for peace of mind and affluence, or is the soul insisting on reaching toward mastery? We not only have to learn to stand up to life and how to form and shape its courses, but we have to become more and more in tune with the subtle currents of Divine Love and Will that work in strange ways. Strangeness always piques our curiosity, and that curiosity is the grace of God calling us to come up higher, know more, find a higher center of balance and stability, and yet remain actively involved in the world of people and things."

Elana R. says that we should work on a regular program of scientific prayer—the proper method depending on the individual—until we achieve greater balance in life. "If an individual is experiencing a pressing need, it may be difficult at first to let go and let the grace of God come forth as the needed thing. Because our mentalities are geared to formulas and techniques, it may be propitious to follow a treatment sequence of choosing, visualizing and affirming until the particular desire is fulfilled. At some point in the development of consciousness, though, the individual will turn within to experience the wholeness of the God-Nature . . . to center the attention exclusively on the Christ Self and let the law outpicture the Truth of that Self."

Daniel E. agreed, saying that "the ritual of treating for things and situations will take a man along the broad avenues of the Path, but when the road becomes straight and narrow, it will be necessary to seek the Kingdom and let all things be added."

It seems that the program outlined in Chapter Six will take us into Phase Five, but if we are to step out into mastery—into the realm of the Supermind—the deeper powers of man must be trained and brought into action. Let's see what the Master Superbeing has to say about this ultimate goal.

"When man comes to himself and comprehends the fact that he is son of God, and knows that in himself lies all the powers of God, he is a master mind and all the elements will hear his voice and gladly do his will"—said the Christ through Jesus. He continues, saying that Fear and Unbelief bind the will of man. "When these are caught and turned aside, the will of man will know no bounds; then man has but to speak and it is done."[1]

Let's analyze these statements.

"When man comes to himself and comprehends the fact that he is son of God . . ." Is he not talking about a realization of Truth? Is he not saying that man *is* a son of God, but that he must understand this fact? If man is to "come to himself"—he must awaken to his true identity. He must understand Who and What he is. And Jesus did not say "if" man comes to himself. He said *when*! This brings in an element of time—in other words, it is only a matter of time until man will awaken from mortal slumber and see himself as he is in Truth, a son of God.

With this realization, man will know *"that in himself lies all the powers of God . . ."* The mystics, the Superbeings have found twelve God-powers within man . . . the Power of *Life*, the Power of *Love*, the Power of *Wisdom*, the Power of *Understanding*, the Power of *Authority*, the

[1] Section XVI, Chapter 92, Verse 11–12, *The Aquarian Gospel of Jesus the Christ*—The Philosophic and Practical Basis of the Religion of the Aquarian Age of the World, Transcribed from the Akashic Records by LEVI. Devorss & Co., Publishers.

Power of *Strength*, the Power of *Order*, the Power of *Faith*, the Power of *Forgiveness*, the Power of *Enthusiasm*, the Power of *Imagination*, and the Power of *Will*. These Powers are etched deeply in the soul of each individual and must be stirred into action if man is to regain his rightful position in the divine scheme of things.

Again—how do we achieve the level of a master mind? By realizing our true identity. How do we bring forth this realization? If we follow Jesus' instruction, we must catch and turn aside fear and unbelief, which "bind the will of man." Now the opposite of fear and unbelief is *Faith*—which also happens to be one of our inherent Powers—so Faith is the Power of the master mind. It is the key to the Kingdom.

Faith is another word that leaves many people a little cold, primarily because they think of it as an anemic concept—a rejection of reasoning. To others, it is used as an excuse, a scapegoat, the object of finger-pointing when prayer does not work. A woman once told me that the biggest problem with prayer was that you "have to have too much faith to make it work, and when I'm hurting, I just can't believe enough to make the pain go away." Many of us give up in despair because we feel that our lack of faith has closed the door to the good that we so desperately seek.

What we do not understand is that we already have all the faith we could possibly need, but we must learn how to use it. Faith is a light of living intelligence and power within the soul . . . it is a thinking entity within your consciousness now . . . and if it is not functioning properly, it is because you have not trained it to do your bidding. This you must do, for Faith is the power that can unite all the other powers of man in a perfect pattern of mastery and dominion. Faith can dissolve the cords that bind the will of man, and when the spiritual center of

Will is free, the Power of Authority is also released and "man has but to speak and it is done."

You already possess the Gift of Faith, because it is one of the attributes of God individualized within you, as you. But you must call this spiritual faculty into expression—into purposeful action in your life.

Pause for a moment and contemplate the idea of Faith. What does it mean to you? Define it. Hold it in your mind and examine evey detail of it. *Faith*! It is the Power that can make you whole, that can move mountains. It is the "substance of things hoped for, the evidence of things not seen." (Heb. II, 11:1) We have been told that ". . . faith subdued kingdoms, wrought righteousness, obtained promises, stopped the mouths of lions, quenched the violence of fire, escaped the edge of the sword . . ." (Heb. II, 11:33–34) Literally, you can do all things through faith because faith is the connecting link between heaven and earth, between cause and effect. The powerful energy of faith will break down the middle wall of partition. The incredibly awesome force of this power will penetrate into the depths of consciousness and burn away the hardened strata of error thought (fear and unbelief). Faith is the foundation upon which the realization of Truth must be built. Remember that your Superconsciousness is whole and complete, but your subconscious mind must be redeemed. It must be restored to its original "Grand Design." The error thoughts must be replaced with concepts of Truth, and it is through the activity of the Power Centers within your soul that the "imprisoned splendor" will be released.

When you call the Power of Faith into expression, it attracts universal energy and substance to become a powerful inner force. When it reaches spiritual maturity it begins its work to restore the subconscious mind to its original state of spiritual consciousness—to be in harmony with your superconsciousness. When—and not if—this happens, you can speak the word and it shall not return unto you void. Your desires will be automatically fulfilled, and your service to mankind shall not be limited to the mind of flesh.

Faith is indeed the key to mastery because it represents all that you are in Truth. Say to yourself with feeling:

I choose to believe that I am more than human. I choose to believe that I am a spiritual being, created in the image and likeness of God. I choose to believe that the Infinite Presence and Power of the Universe has individualized as me, as the Reality of me, as my true nature. I believe that all that the Father is, I am, and all that the Father has is mine. I believe that the I AM of me is God in expression, a consciousness of power and dominion. I believe that I AM the Knowledge of Truth, therefore, I AM the Faith of God made manifest. I AM FAITH. I know that God knows my every need, and that it is His good pleasure to restore the lost years of the locust, to straighten out every crooked place, to perfect all that concerns me, and to make all things new in my life. I know that He has already done this by giving me the Gift of Himself, which is my all-sufficiency. I know that through this spiritual treatment, my belief in all that is good and true is entering my subconscious mind, where it is being clothed with spiritual power, substance, life and intelligence. Because I AM Faith, I HAVE Faith, and I feel the spiritual energy of Faith throughout my being now. I will care for my Faith, feeding it with thoughts of the Kingdom, of the Power, and the Glory. In my heart it will grow strong and vibrant and powerful, and will move quickly to unite with its True Self, the Spirit of Truth, my very own Superconsciousness. I will then behold myself as I am in Truth . . . the Christ, Son of the Living God. And it is so.

Your consciousness is your Faith

The stream of thoughts that continually flow through your mind come from your faith faculty. Remember, these are not *your* thoughts. They are the words and images of this living, thinking entity within you called Faith. Since this entity is one of *your* powers, it belongs to *you*, and it must be under your control, your management, your supervision. When it sends forth thoughts of lack, limitation, failure, futility, loneliness or illness, you must discipline it immediately, because its word is law and it can hold you in negative circumstances unless you take command. Do not condemn it, though. Understand that it has been operating in accordance with appearances for longer than you can imagine, so you must direct its focus to the Christ-Truth within. But once it recognizes the Christ, it will become the organizing center for all of your other powers.

Faith is the "thinking" center in your mind, and according to the Superbeings, that energy center is located in the center of the brain. Its energy waves flow through the brain continuously and if you are not in control, Faith can lead you into a far country like the prodigal son. But after you have begun to assume control of this faculty, you will notice periods of great joy with no obvious explanation. What has happened is that Faith has touched the Order Center within your consciousness and you feel that all is "right and good." At other times you'll feel the energy of great enthusiasm, and you will know that Faith is in contact with this faculty. A great warm feeling of love will also signify that Faith is in communication with your Love Center—and the next time you are complimented on a marvelously wise decision, just pause a moment and thank your Faith entity for its work with your Wisdom Center.

Faith is constantly feeding the other Power Centers

with "food" that it is accepting as true. This is why you must teach it to concentrate on Truth thoughts, and when its mind wanders to reflect on negative appearances, call it back to view things from the highest vision. Since Faith is your thinking power, its thoughts must be trained to be loving, wise, enthusiastic, powerful, strong, forgiving, orderly, understanding, imaginative, filled with life and in tune with the will of God. Then all the power centers will be united and your subconscious will be filled with the Light of Spirit.

Faith has a very close affinity with three other power centers—Strength, Wisdom and Love—and when it begins to interact with these particular faculties, the expansion of consciousness is greatly increased. But you must speak the word:

> Come, Faith, follow me. It is upon you that I will build my spiritual consciousness. You shall be a rock, and the firmness of my solid belief in the Christ Truth shall be the foundation for my consciousness of mastery. Through the activity of your Knowingness, I shall achieve the dominion that is my birthright. You will fill my mind with rich, abiding substance. You will fill my thoughts with the presence of God. You will fill my emotions with the love of God. You will fill my words with the power of God. You will fill my actions with the energy of God so that nothing shall be impossible to me.
>
> My Faith, the Spirit of Living Faith within me, is strong and wise and loving—and it now assists me in calling forth the Powers of Strength, Wisdom and Love.
>
> I place my Faith in the Strength that I AM. Come forth, Strength, I call you into action.
>
> I place my Faith in the Wisdom that I AM. Come forth, Wisdom, into perfect expression.

I place my Faith in the Love that I AM. Come forth, Love, and radiate forever throughout my being.

Through the activity of Faith, Strength, Wisdom and Love, I now embark on a journey toward Christhood. And it is so!

Review Your Desire List

If your needs are financial, meditate on these words until they become real to you:

I place my faith in the Christ Mind within, knowing that it is even now interpreting itself as my abundant supply. It moves easily through my faith to manifest as my all-sufficiency. I see my desires being fulfilled quickly and in peace. It is done!

If your body requires healing, say:

I place my faith in the Christ Mind within, knowing that it is even now erasing every pattern of disease in my subconscious mind and restoring the patterns of perfect health. My faith opens the way for the healing work of Spirit, and I am healed. I see this Truth. I feel it. Therefore, it is done!

Place your faith in the indwelling Christ and call forth the fulfillment of each of your other desires. Keep working daily and move up to a level of "no concern." Make your demonstration and move past the acute trials and tribulations of daily living. Then, as your consciousness expands, your work to demonstrate one particular good will not be necessary. A treatment for a specific thing or experience will not be required—because you will be working to demonstrate faith in your God-Self, your True Self, in order to bring forth all the good that God has for you now. You will be taking the Christ within, your True Self, as your All-Sufficiency. You will rely on

115

Him and only Him to make all the adjustments in your life according to His Plan for you—and to bring the fullness of that plan into expression here and now. Instead of enjoying little pieces of the Kingdom bit by bit, you will let the whole Kingdom of God be your inheritance. *This is The Ultimate Way!*

Once you move to the point in consciousness where you pass the anxiety stage of "need"—your only responsibility will be to manage the Power of Faith—to see that this holy helper stays on the job to keep the channel open. He shall be the "lamp of the Lord" . . . the instrument through which the Power flows. So as quickly as you can, turn your attention from the needs of the outer world to the inner force of Faith and let your other Super-Powers unite in perfect harmony.

You Shall Speak the Word

Remember, when fear and unbelief are "caught and turned aside, the will of man will know no bounds; then man has but to speak and it is done." This means that through the action of Faith, working with the faculties of Strength, Wisdom and Love, your Will center will be freed of the personal ego and will turn its attention to the Will of your Superconsciousness, the Christ. Your Authority center will automatically react to this shift in focus and your words will take on new power to shape events, circumstances and experiences in your life. But Creative Mind made sure that when the Authority center was stimulated, there was also a triggering response in the Understanding faculty to bring it into play at the same time. Otherwise, the power of Authority would be strictly in the hands of a predominately "human" consciousness and would be like a child playing with fire.

But with Authority and Understanding combined, the remaining powers now unite in divine sequence. Great enthusiasm is generated, which stirs the imagination. Through the Imagination faculty and the ability to "see" clearly the fulfillment of every desire, order is established in your life and affairs. There is great joy now, and your soul is filled with forgiveness toward everyone and everything. You feel the Life Force of the Living Christ pulsating through every fiber of your being, and you know that you are now experiencing the realities of your spiritual nature.

"When man comes to himself and comprehends the fact that he is son of God, and knows that in himself lies all the powers of God . . ."

The powers of God are *your* powers. They have been given to every man to help him "come to himself." Make the exciting discovery of these powerful forces within you now. They are asleep and must be awakened. Spend time every day calling forth each one as Jesus called forth Lazarus—then contemplate each Power Center within you for several minutes.

O Faith, awake! I now place my faith in the Power of Faith that I AM. I AM FAITH.

O Strength, awake! I now place my faith in the Power of Strength that I AM. I AM STRENGTH.

O Wisdom, awake! I now place my faith in the Power of Wisdom that I AM. I AM WISDOM.

O Love, awake! I now place my faith in the Power of Love that I AM. I AM LOVE.

O Will, awake! I now place my faith in the Power of Will that I AM. I AM WILL.

O Authority, awake! I now place my faith in the Power of Authority that I AM. I AM AUTHORITY.

O Understanding, awake! I now place my faith in the

Power of Understanding that I AM. I AM UNDER-STANDING.

O Enthusiasm, awake! I now place my faith in the Power of Enthusiasm that I AM. I AM ENTHUSIASM.

O Imagination, awake! I now place my faith in the Power of Imagination that I AM. I AM IMAGINATION.

O Order, awake! I now place my faith in the Power of Order that I AM. I AM ORDER.

O Forgiveness, awake! I now place my faith in the Power of Forgiveness that I AM. I AM FORGIVENESS.

O Life, awake! I now place my faith in the Power of Life that I AM. I AM LIFE.

I now place my Faith in the Truth. I know that I am a Son of God, created in the image and likeness of the Father, and I am now continuously aware of Who and What I AM.

Now say to yourself:
"I have come to myself and I now comprehend the fact that I am a son of God, and I know that in myself lie all the powers of God. I am a master mind and all the elements hear my voice and gladly do my will. Fear and unbelief, which have bound my will, have been caught and turned aside. Now my will knows no bounds, and I have but to speak and it is done. And it is so!"

When your subconscious mind believes that you are all that God is in expression, it has no choice but to stop believing everything else to the contrary. The inner chambers of your mind will then be filled with the Light of Truth, and your whole outer world—beginning with your body—will become a perfect reflection of the Light. Health, wealth, success, achievement, love and companionship, protection, strength and vitality, joy and order, guidance, individual freedom, and wonderful service to others will be yours.

But you cannot get from where you are now to where you want to be by wishing, hoping, or even praying in the traditional way. The way to mastery is through a dedication to the principles of Truth, and by embodying these principles in your consciouness. You begin by tapping the power of Faith, and through daily meditation, bringing all your Super-Powers into alignment with the Christ Mind within. This is the redeeming of your subconscious mind. This is achieving the "mind-of-one-vibration." This is The Ultimate Way!

Then, when you least expect it, the Dawning will come and you will know Who you are. You will be in the realm of the Supermind where YOU will assist in mankind's evolution.

In truth, that is why you are here.

APPENDIX

The Quartus
Foundation

The Quartus Foundation is an organization dedicated to research and communications on the human potential. We seek to study the records of the past, investigate events and experiences of the present, and probe the possibilities and potential of the future through the illumined consciousness of the Advanced Souls.

Our objective is to continually document the truth that man is a spiritual being possessing all of the powers of the spiritual realm . . . that man is indeed God individualized . . . and that as man realizes his true identity, he becomes a Master Mind with dominion over the material world.

The documentation comes through indepth research into case histories of the past and present, which reveal the healing, prospering, harmonizing Power of God working in and through man. We believe that man is capable of rising above every problem and challenge that could possibly beset him, and that he is doing this daily in ways that are considered both "mysterious and miraculous." But in truth, the evil, the illness, the failure, the limitation, the danger, the injustice disappear through a change in individual consciousness. What brought about the change? What steps were taken to raise the consciousness above the level of the difficulty? What were the sequence of events in the revelation of harmony? How was consciousness able to literally reshape, reconstruct and readjust the outer scene? Was it not the Power of God in action through the mind of man?

We seek to examine closely the problem and the solution, the activity of Mind and the Law of Mind, the cause and effect—and to build a fund of knowledge based on the interrelationship of spirit, soul, body, and the world of form and experience.

We believe that what one person is doing to alter conditions and reveal order and harmony, all can do—and by researching and communicating specific examples of man's inherent powers, we can do our part in assisting in the general upliftment of consciousness. Through greater understanding of the human potential, we can all develop a more dynamic faith in our inner Self . ... a conviction that our potential is only limited by the scope of our vision . . . and a Knowlede that mankind is Godkind—and does not have to accept anything less than heaven on earth.

You can help us in our research, because the very fact that you have read this book is an indication that you are on an evolving path toward a higher consciousness. "And with every degree of change . . ." you will see a corresponding effect in your world and affairs, so we invite you to share your experiences with us in strictest confidence and participate in our program. Remember

". . . as you share (your) experiences with others, and as they share their experiences with you, you will grow together. You, and others who will join you in the journey, are seeking the Fourth Dimensional Consciousness, which was established within all mankind in the beginning."

—Page xxii, Author's Preface

The Quartus Foundation is also forming a *Council of Masters* composed of Illumined Ones—those with a predominantly spiritual consciousness. We are asking these masters to reveal to us—according to the level of their understanding—additional insights, explanations, opinions and predictions on such subjects as the Divine Plan for each individual life, Dreams, Family Life, the future of this Planet, Heredity, International Relations, Life after Death, Life in Other Worlds, Parenting, Prayer, Soul Mates, Spiritual Healing, and many, many other topics of major importance to each individual, to our country, and to the world in which we live. And again, we wish to share this information with you.

For complete details on the activities of The Quartus Foundation, write for your free copy of the Quartus Report, P. O. Box 26683, Austin, Texas 78755.

Use this book as a manual for the training of consciousness, and keep a record of the changes that take place in your life.

Make notes on the pages that follow of your demonstrations of the Power at work. Later, transfer your notes to a private notebook and develop your own Spiritual Diary.

Remember, whether or not you achieve your heart's desires is strictly up to you. The choice is yours, so begin now to bring your life up to the level of your highest vision.

PERSONAL NOTES

PERSONAL NOTES

PERSONAL NOTES

PERSONAL NOTES

PERSONAL NOTES

PERSONAL NOTES

PERSONAL NOTES

PERSONAL NOTES